THE EMBEDDED INTERNET:
The Final Evolution!

by **WALLY WOOD**

Foreword by
Elmo Wright
"Father of the Touchdown Spike & End-Zone Dance*"*
Kansas City Chiefs
Wide-Receiver
1971-75

"The Internet is about to go underground and behind sealed walls. It's destined to be attached to everything you touch ... And to everything that touches you!"

A Life of Consistency

by Elmo Wright
"Father of the Touchdown Spike & the End-Zone Dance"
U of H *Cougar* Wide Receiver - 1969-70
All-America Team - 1970
1971 First-round draft pick, Kansas City Chiefs (1971-75)

I don't remember exactly when it was that I first met Wally Wood, but I know it was in the mid- to late 1970s. He was working for a local Radio Shack store at the time. I came into the store to buy some sound equipment supplies and he was the salesman who greeted me and offered to help me.

We just got to talking, first about the kind of entertainment equipment I was interested in at the time and then some other matters. The conversation eventually drifted to certain world issues that were important at the time, and Wally found himself explaining to me the future of world politics and economics. Consequently, he ended up telling me about the cashless society and one world government, and how these things would likely be true as we crossed into the next century.

Well, I don't mind telling you that it didn't make a lot of sense to me at the time. I was preparing to go off to the National Football League to pursue my dream of professional football ... and, here's this stranger in a stereo shop talking to me about world politics and a futuristic economic system of no cash. It was too heavy for me at the time.

But, he *was* persuasive, I'll give him that much. I don't remember how long we visited, but I have remembered that visit to this day, over 20 years later.

After that day, I may have seen him once or twice more before he was transferred to another store, and then it would be 10 years more before I saw him again. On that occasion, I was shopping at a local grocery store. In fact, I was actually checking out through the grocery line when, who should I see working in the Photo Lab department but my old friend. Funny — at the precise moment I saw him, I was pulling out my debit card to pay my grocery bill. Suddenly, I heard the words *"cashless society"* go off in my head. I had to laugh out loud. I hadn't thought of that phrase in some 10 years. Now, I'm actively participating in it in the very store that Wally is working at. The irony of it all simply floored me.

Now, some 15 years after *that* incident, I find myself crossing paths with Wally from time to time, and we often speak of those things ... of how the years have, among other things, produced the exact unfolding of events as Wally had told me over 20 years ago would happen. How did he know *then* what course our world would take as we headed for the new millennium?

What has always impressed me about him is how very sure he has always been about these things. He has always spoken as one who knows for sure, without a shadow of doubt, that these things were going to happen, and that they were going to happen in *"our"* lifetime! How does he know these things with such certainty? It never ceases to amaze me.

Let me invite you to read this book that my friend has written. Even I don't claim to fully understand all that he says here, but you will never find *me* arguing or taking issue with his perspective. I've been a longtime witness — and beneficiary — of his track record in these matters. He got my attention back in the '70s, and I have lived to see it begin to come to pass. I hope you will "hear" it, too.

— ***Elmo Wright***
July 1999

The Next Evolution of the World Wide Web

"Consider that in less than 50 years, computers have gone from monstrosities the size of a living room to small working units weighing a few ounces to a few pounds at most that we tote with us in our briefcases or wear on our belts. The Internet is swiftly replacing the shopping mall, and email is more common than a neighbor's wave. The Melissa virus and the year 2000 bug have hammered home the realization that *computers control everything* — from grocery checkouts and bank machines to global communications, air transportation and the world's financial structure," reports the cover story article, "Virtual Certainty: Films Reflect Computer Fears," in the April 21, 1999 edition of *USA Today*.

"Forget the futuristic plots on the big screen. Even today, the not-so-virtual reality is we can't disconnect HAL (the ubiquitous super-computer villain of *2000: A Space Odyssey*). We need him too much!"

- - - - - - - - - - - - - - - -

Syndicated columnist for the *Chicago Tribune*, Mike Royco, in his March 24, 1996 column entitled "How to Eavesdrop — by Computer," told the story of Marcia, a single mother, and an experience she had involving her son's computer. Her ex-husband wanted to set up a computer with Internet access so he and the boy could stay in touch via email and chat rooms. Marcia saw no threat in this, so she gave her approval.

Royko writes: "One day, the son came home after visiting his dad's place. He casually mentioned: 'Mama, guess what? I heard your voice through Daddy's computer!'"

It turns out that dear old Dad had pulled a fast one on Marcia by installing a particular software into the son's computer that made it possible for him, the Dad, to dial in and take control of the son's computer. "Then," Marcia explained, "my son's computer picks up sounds in my house and transmits them back to (my ex-husband's) computer," where they are played over his system's multimedia speakers.

In following up her find, Marcia discovered that "there is a divorced men's group on the Internet, and they give each other advice about how, if a man is in a custody battle for the children, this is a way to get the goods on your wife," she said.

"The reason I'm telling you this," she concluded, "is that computers can be wonderful things. But people should be aware that they can be dangerous, too. In a situation where a divorce is acrimonious, they can be an effective form of eavesdropping."

As Royko himself checked out her story, he found that this type of "poor man's espionage" is relatively easy to do ... though somewhat expensive. He was told by one computer specialist: "If she has a voice-data modem on the computer, what happens is it has a duplex speaker phone on it. By accessing her computer and activating the modem and speaker phone, anything in microphone range can be picked up and the person on the other end can hear it."

Here We Are ... Trapped!

Welcome to the world of *ubiquitous computing* ... where once private lives now live in glass houses ... where hidden technology exposes *everything* to the light of knowledge and information ... where deception and manipulation become the by-products to the command: "Enter your PIN number, please."

In the *Forward* to David Burnham's book, THE RISE OF THE COMPUTER STATE, renowned television news anchor Walter Cronkite writes, "(George) Orwell, with his vivid imagination, was unable to foresee the actual shape of the threat that would exist (in our day). It turns out to be the *ubiquitous* computer and its ancillary communications networks. Without the malign intent of any government system or would-be dictator, our privacy is being invaded, and more and more of the experiences which should be solely our own are finding their way into electronic files that the curious can scrutinize at the punch of a button.

"If — or is it *when?*" he concludes, "these computers are permitted to talk to one another, when they are interlinked, they can spew out a roomful of data on each of us that will leave us naked before whoever gains access to the information."

Going Underground and Behind Walls

Our entry into Huxley's *Brave New World* of Orwell's *1984* is just about to cross the "point of no return" — across the threshold of ubiquity!

What is *ubiquity*? According to Random House Webster's College Dictionary (Random House, 1992), it is the state of "existing or being everywhere, especially at the same time; *omnipresent.*"

Omnipresent! Isn't that what is considered to be a "Divine attribute" alongside *omnipotence* (infinite power and authority) and *omniscience* (infinite knowledge)? In a world of man-made technology, how does this translate?

"The goal of *ubiquitous computing* is the production of devices that are so commonplace and natural to use that they become almost invisible." So wrote the students of Virginia Tech's Department of Computer Science in their 1998 book, WORLD WIDE WEB: BEYOND THE BASICS (Prentice Hall, New Jersey).

"The term *ubiquitous* means that there will be hundreds of tiny computers in an office or home, each doing its own specialized task," they wrote.

In the World of Ubiquity, computers everywhere are linked invisibly to people everywhere and things everywhere. The resultant network of ever-flowing information becomes one massive, global "living" entity ... the ultimate in the theology of evolution — the marriage of man and machine!

Tracks in the Cybersand

Alexander Solzhenitsyn, world renowned Soviet dissident and political author of the 1970s, gave these words in a college commencement speech, addressing modern man's bondage to information: "As every man goes through life, he fills in a number of forms for the record, each containing a number of questions. There are thus hundreds of little threads radiating from man — millions of threads in all. If these threads were suddenly to become visible, people would lose all ability to move."

From his book, INFORMATION WARFARE (Thunder's Mouth Press, New York), privacy expert and cyberspace specialist Winn Schwartau writes: "An estimated three billion computers run every aspect of our lives. These computers aren't quite so obvious to us because they tend to be invisibly enmeshed into the fabric of our daily chores. These billions of computers, plus the hundred million-plus business-oriented computer systems, are what we call *Computers Everywhere*. They are indeed everywhere.

"We can no longer ignore the impact of Computers Everywhere on Everyman and Everywoman. Billions of computers are invisibly embedded in almost everything we do. Computers Everywhere will only increase!"

Film historian and critic Leonard Maltin, in speaking on today's genre of *virtual certainty* films, was quoted in the April 21, 1999 edition of *USA Today* as saying, "Computers have just become such a pervasive part of our society ... We are still uncomfortable with what computers represent, the loss of control of our lives. We want computers to help us, not rule us. They are supposed to be a tool, a slave, not our masters."

Once again ... Welcome — to the world of transparent living and translucent lives spent within the glass walls of an open society controlled by the ubiquitous computing of an embedded global information system ... that will look like and act like an apocryphal *beast!*

Introduction - The Next Evolution

- - - - - - - - - - - - - - -

"The Internet is here to stay. It is transforming technology. It will alter the way business, commerce, medicine, science, communications, the law, politics and government are conducted. The Internet changes everything it touches, and it touches almost everything."

— John Ellis
Boston Globe

The world is changing rapidly. The globalization of the economy, the fact that <u>*we live from now on in an information society*</u> (emphasis added), the complexity and the uncertainty which are the common trademarks of the present world lead us to take into consideration a number of these new factors. We have to understand these new data in order to have a better understanding of other cultures, other languages, other modes of reasoning.

"The New Global Society" webpage
http://www.clubofrome.org/globis_nsoc.htm

The Ever-Growing Internet

- There are over 200 countries and territories with access to the Internet of one kind or another, although it varies in penetration.

  Vint Cerf,
  "father of the Internet"
  Dallas Morning News
  Tues. Feb. 16, 1999

- Approximately 52,000 Americans sign on to the Internet as new users each day.

  Vice President Al Gore,
  White House Internet
  Conference, November 1998

- According to market researcher Cahners In-Stat Group, by 2003 the "home network" market will have reached 1.4 billion homes, representing a growth of more than 600 percent. In America, there are over 21 million homes with more than one PC.

  Current Technology, Mar 99;
  "Home Networking Could
  Skyrocket Within Five Years."

- More than 3. 4 trillion e-mail messages crossed the Internet in the United States in 1998, as compared with 107 billion First Class "snail mail" pieces at that same time by the US Post Office.

  Emarketer, Inc.
  A market research group

▸ "The PC penetration rate continues to increase at a healthy clip, showing that the PC is rapidly becoming a standard household appliance. There is evidence that the first-time buyers are coming from households in the lower socio-economic levels. However, the increase in penetration is across all segments."

Van Baker
director/Consumer Market Group
Dataquest, Inc.

▸ Revenues from Internet-based advertising have grown to the point where they have already broken the $1 billion mark for much of 1998.

PricewaterhouseCoopers
Internet Advertising Bureau survey

▸ Half of all U.S. homes at the close of 1998 owned at least one personal computer, and one-third of all these were online on the Internet.

Homefront survey conducted by
research firm, **Odyssey**

Challenge —

"And he had power to give life unto the image of the beast, that the image of the beast should both speak, and cause as many as would not worship the image of the beast should be killed. "

—Revelation 13:15

Here is a biblical prophecy "for the end times" that speaks of a global administration that would be so powerful, so encompassing, so all-consuming, that it would have the power to kill those who do not obey its every command. In a world of 6 billion people, how are they going to know who's worshiping and who's not?

Preface - The Ever-Growing Internet

The answer is found in realizing that, in order to *rule* the world, there is the corresponding need to *control* the world. This is made possible in the advancing technologies of a global super-high tech communication network.

Before moving forward, however, it's important that the reader be warned: This will prove to be a treatise of strange mix — bringing together two seemingly different worlds: high-tech communications and global politics. In this particular instance, there is definitely a clear correlation between the two.

Welcome to the world of the Internet!

- - - - - - - - - - - - - - - -

The Internet, like the personal computer (PC), is the fastest growing technology ever in the history of man. Both separate and together, both of these phenomenons have outpaced every new technology development of the twentieth century! And, before the next century is even half-a-decade old, even *this* technology promises to be changed all the more in ways unimaginable to anyone outside the realm of science fiction. The best of Isaac Asimov, Aldus Huxley, and George Orwell will have teamed with that of Tom Clancy and John Grisham in the next phase of *technoevolution* ... The Embedded Internet!

"We are making the transition into a new era of computing," writes Michael J. Miller, editor-in-chief for *PC Magazine* in his May 26, 1998 article entitled, "The Fifth Age of Computing."

"The signs of this new era are everywhere," he continues. "The combination of the Internet and new devices signals the shift into the era of Ubiquitous Computing ... the Fifth Age of Computing.

"In this new era, we'll each use all sorts of devices. Each device will have more computing power than the PCs of the 1980s or the mainframes of the 1960s and 1970s. The devices will have to work independently, but they will also have to be able to communicate with one another."

What's he talking about? What's this *"new era"* he's talking about? Ubiquitous computing? — what's that? I don't like the sound of that.

Should I be concerned?

And, this thing about smarter devices that have "more computing power" than all the hi-tech desktops and mainframes that went before. What's that all about? What kinds of devices? How will these "devices" be more powerful than today's PCs that can launch a rocket into outer space and then, through advanced robotics, manage the rocketed payload once it gets there?

Then, if *that* wasn't enough, listen to Miller's next comment: "More crucial information than ever will be stored in large databases managed by IT (Information Technology) departments." In other words, more dossiers and more gathered information with which and through which we are easily tracked ... right? Is that where this new era is taking us — right smack into the arms of George Orwell's *1984*? Is that what this is all about — the final chapter of man's long earthly saga in which he, indeed, finds himself hopelessly enslaved to that super politician and global technogeek known historically as Big Brother ... "the last Caesar" *... the Antichrist?!*

This book attempts to show the likelihood of that very thing happening as this new era begins soon. Without the aid of this author's subjective opinions, a potpourri of authors cascade through the following chapters from the paragraphs of their own writings, observations and conclusions about (1) what *kind* of technology is coming around the next corner, and (2) *where* that technology is likely to take us.

Here's just a small sampling of what awaits the reader: David Burnham's *The Rise of the Computer State* (1984); *The Telematic Society* by England's foremost IBMer, James Martin (1981); one of MIT's many technogurus, Michael Dertouzos, in his 1997 book, *What Will Be: How the New World of Information Will Change Our Lives*; also *The Shape of Things to Come* (1999) by Vanderbilt University's Richard W. Oliver (a *BusinessWeek* book); and William Greider, national editor for *Rolling Stone* magazine, from his window on the world treatise, *One World: Ready or Not!* (1997, Simon & Schuster).

And, then, there are such publications and website news articles as *Wired, TIME, WorldNetDaily, Popular Science, ABCNews.com,*

ComputerWorld, Auto I.D News, The Industry Standard, Fortune, PC Magazine, InfoWorld and literally dozens more of high caliber and recognizable credibility.

The belabored point is this: the *world* is telling us where the *world* is taking us. Not only are many of the world's staunchest observers telling us what is coming, but they are also starting to ask some very pointed, poignant questions. Is it possible that it is no longer just the pastors, preachers and prophets who are warning that the world (or, at least, *our* world as we know it) is coming to an end? Could it also be that the politicians, pundits and power brokers are observing something akin to the same? Are they *all* wrong in what they are telling us they are seeing?

Why write this book? Because the changes that are coming *are coming!* It's an absolute fact before it gets here. This book is intended to be a trumpet of warning ... for all the *convenience* that will be overplayed in the marketing and the propaganda attached to the new technology of the embedded Internet and its myriad peripherals, there is *still* a darker side to it all that will not be discussed or mentioned by the promoters of the new era.

From the very beginning, a spin cycling campaign will emerge designed to immediately and mercilessly undermine and torpedo any efforts to present an alternative perspective to the benefits that will be promised ... a perspective that will unveil more truth about the direction and intentions of the new technology than any of its designers would care to have exposed.

In historical terms, the new technology that is coming will be a *Trojan horse.* Presented as a gift to the *Jetsons* generation, it will, in due course and at the appropriate moment, release its inner terror upon an unsuspecting, naive, *sleeping* world.   *— WW*

Table of Contents

University of Houston football great — "father of the *End-Zone Dance.*" Wright has known the author since the late 1970s.

The destiny of the Internet has always been focused on linking people to computers — literally! The *Information Super-highway* was to always be a conduit over which all human activity would be traceable, trackable, viewable. The future is now! The "final evolution" of telecommunication technology is now beyond the drawing board, coming to a retail shelf near you soon.

National and international facts and figures of how broad and deep the growth of the Internet has been. "We are making the transition into a new era of computing," writes the editor of *PC Magazine*. *"The signs of this new era are everywhere ... the Fifth Age of Computing."*

"We're creating a *new society*," writes Alvin Toffler. *"A new civilization is emerging in our lives bring(ing)with it new family styles, changed ways of working, loving and living; a new economy; new political conflicts ... the Third Wave!"* How is a growing Internet contributing to this new society?

The *Invisible* Internet

As a "global network of networks," the Net is going *ubiquitous* — underground and behind closed walls, attached to everything we touch and everything that touches us! As *Newsweek* magazine reports, "Everything is going on the Net. Everything!"

The Loss of Privacy in an Over-Networked World

"The law right now does not look good for privacy plaintiffs," writes Arkansas University law professor Andrew McClurg, in his 1992 study into privacy issues. Indeed, as David Brin points out in his 1998 book, TRANSPARENT SOCIETY, "it is already too late to prevent the invasion of cameras and databases. No matter how many laws are passed, it will prove quite impossible to legislate away the new surveillance tools and databases. They are here to stay. Light *is* going to shine into nearly every corner of our lives."

The R&D of the U.C.E.   **51**

Starting in late-1999, the research and development of the *ubiquitous computing era's* consumer products with Internet access are circulating the globe. Do your on-line banking via your kitchen microwave oven. Want to order another gallon of ice cream? Simply scan the half-empty carton you have over the code reading scanner built into your refrigerator-freezer, and your order should arrive first thing in the morning. Are you one of those who has trouble remembering names and faces? No more. Not if you're wearing database glasses from MIT or PC clothing from IBM.

Just within the average home alone, there are literally dozens of items that are destined to be linked to the *elements* of ubiquity, making them the *products* of ubiquity ... creating interactive ubiquitous *zones* within the home. The kitchen, the family room, the bedroom, the study, the bath and, yes, even the closets; they are all future recipients of Internet connection.

Where is all this new era progress taking us? What does it all mean? What's on the other side where there awaits another millennia of mind-defying hi-tech development? Can we be guaranteed that there will <u>*never, ever*</u> be another Hitler, Stalin or Mao Tse-tung who won't seize the opportunity of gaining more hi-tech divinity than all of history's despots combined?

As was noted in Chapter 1, the fact that the Internet is going embedded in a very short while is indication that there is the need for centralization in due course. But, centralized into what? The point is: there *is* an agenda ... a goal and direction to it all. The challenge will be whether or not we will like all the changes that are destined to take place in this brave, bold new world of ubiquitous technology.

Late-breaking news supportive to the theme of this treatise.

It Wants to Live, Grow
and Evolve ... *Toward What?*

Gina Smith, computer editor for ABC's *"Good Morning, America!"* and syndicated columnist for *Popular Science* magazine, in an article entitled "A Smaller Net" (PS, Feb. 1996), wrote: "The Internet is seemingly everywhere ... it has become THE clearinghouse for the world's messages, linking virtually all of the planet's public and private networks. It's an astoundingly important development. It will likely remain — and evolve — as the premier communications medium of our time."

For as popular as the Internet has become, everywhere one looks and reads these days, the most common observation from a myriad of circles is: *The Internet is alive ... it wants to grow ... it will continue to evolve!* It's hard enough to see a network of machines as a living, *breathing* species of the non-organic order — but this idea of it *evolving* into something different from what it is now is even harder to comprehend. What *is* the Net evolving into? What are the implications of that evolution? Should we be concerned?

Winn Schwartau, author of INFORMATION WARFARE, has been called "the most dangerous man in America — and the most valuable," by Robert Steele, former Deputy Director of the *United States Marine Corps'* Intelligence Center and current president of Open Source Solutions, Inc. Schwartau describes the Information Superhighway this way: "Today, the Global Network, still in its formative infancy, is a living, breathing entity on planet Earth as much as we are. Our reliance on the Global Network has become so immense that, if the entire Network were turned off, we would literally die. From that perspective, we and the Global Network have become symbiotic (mutual, common). We need it to survive and it wants to grow."

This concept of a *living* network seems to leave open the next logical step in evolutionary thinking — the identity of man himself in light of his own god-like inventions.

From his book, THE AGE OF SPIRITUAL MACHINES: *When Computers Exceed Human Intelligence*, artificial intelligence guru and inventor Ray Kurzweil proclaims: "Before the next century is over, human beings will no longer be the most intelligent or capable type of entity on the planet. Actually, let me take that back. The truth of that last statement depends on how we define *human*. And here we see one profound difference between these two centuries: The primary political and philosophical issue of the next century will be the definition of *who we are*.

"In the second decade of the next century, it will become increasingly difficult to draw any clear distinction between the capabilities of human and machine intelligence. The advantages of computer intelligence in terms of speed, accuracy and capacity will be clear. The advantages of human intelligence, on the other hand, will become increasingly difficult to distinguish."

Kurzweil goes on to say that, early in the coming century, advancements in technology will be of such superior essence that science may well declare such super technology as being "a new form of intelligence on Earth."

"It will be no less important than the creation of the intelligence that created it," he says, "and will have profound implications for all aspects of human endeavor, including the nature of work, human learning, government, warfare, the arts, and *our concept of ourselves*."

Winn Schwartau once again, this time on the elimination of the human factor from the hi-tech equations of this brave new world: "Estimations are that data storage requirements of a large corporation will soon exceed one petabyte, or one billion gigabytes.

"Artificial intelligence systems will have to decide which information is relevant and which is irrelevant; more computers to decide which other computers are worth listening to. Human intervention, even in the decision-making process, will no longer be possible. We will have to trust that the *cyberpriests* develop artificial intelligence machines smart enough — *human* enough — to make decisions with which we are comfortable."

The redefinition of the human factor in a world of evolving artificial intelligence and global computer networks suggests there is a whole new world being shaped and created right before our eyes.

In his blockbuster treatise, FUTURE SHOCK, new age futurist Alvin Toffler writes: "We are creating a new society. Not a changed society. Not an extended, larger-than-life version of our present society. But a *new society.* Unless we understand this, we shall destroy ourselves in trying to cope with tomorrow."

In further defining this new global paradigm, Toffler expands this theme in two other books, giving exact or similar openings in both THE THIRD WAVE and CREATING A NEW CIVILIZATION:

"A new civilization is emerging in our lives, and blind men everywhere are trying to suppress it. This new civilization brings with it new family styles, changed ways of working, loving and living; a new economy; new political conflicts, and beyond all this, an altered consciousness as well.

"Without clearly recognizing it, we are engaged in building a remarkable new civilization from the ground up. This is the meaning of the Third Wave.

"The America we know is dying, but a second America is rising from the body of the first ... America II," writes Richard Louv in AMERICA II.

This Global Network of stockpiled dossiers and real-time communications is changing the face of the world as we have historically known it. The *imaginational* lines that comprise the nation-states are progressively fading away in the light of global electronic funds transfer, automated banking, Iridium-based cell phones, GPS-trackable silicon chips and Internet-connected refrigerators that place hands-free long-distance phone calls to anywhere on earth ... without incurring long-distance charges!

Chapter 1 - It Wants to Evolve

In the late '80s, this reporter worked among the administrators, scientists and astronauts of the Johnson Space Center in Houston, Texas. At the time, I was president of The Shuttle News Service, and was commissioned by new business partners to build the space industry's only dedicated news agency under the auspices of the Space & Telecomm News Bureau.

At that time, Houston was suffering under the throes of what many called an oil industry-induced economic depression for the area. The city was frantically searching for another venue in which to diversify its multifaceted economic base. The space industry was seen as a serious alternative in re-establishing Houston's tarnished image.

Dozens upon dozens of local companies and multinational corporations enjoined themselves to the major contractors and subcontractors of NASA to add the necessary push into the new frontier. "Space Entrepreneurism & Commercialization" was the new theme. "The Oil & Space Capitol" was the new identity for a city teetering on the edge of possibly losing both.

As I ventured among the numerous conferences, workshops, offices, luncheons and test labs, I kept encountering a common theme of discussion. In fact, once I discovered this common theme, it didn't take much to invoke a conversation of idealistic concepts and convictions on this single topic ... *global management!*

Everywhere I went throughout the entire industry, *global management* was easy to talk about. I gathered endless hours of personal interviews of space scientists, engineers, architects and administrators who spend their lives looking at the earth from the *outside* looking in! Reams upon reams of earth-shots from orbiting space craft and from the moon — looking back upon a crystalline blue planet upon which are found no boundaries, no regions, no states, no countries. Nothing more than multi-hued continents separated by oceans and marked by rivers. At night, you see the glimmering jewels of cities and towns where people live ... but no discernible cultures, races or politics.

This, to the average space scientist, IS the *real* world! This is the world that space cameras record, then play back over the projectors and screens of industry luncheons and briefings. Where are the lines that divide us, industry pundits ask. Why is the world so difficult to manage? Why can't it be run like any large corporation in the land today? You don't have life-threatening wars taking place either within or between the multinational corporations of today. You have, instead, corporate peace and harmony administered by a strong central government with only a token hint of democracy to help maintain at least the elusion of unity between the corporate classes (management vs labor).

Former astronauts Joe Allen and Gene Cerran address the media at a news conference hosted by S&T News Bureau during *Vision '87 Space & Telecomm Symposium* in Houston, June 9, 1987. Seated is Wally Wood, Bureau Chief of Space & Telecomm News Bureau (STN).

Why can't such realities be installed and applied to our much-tortured, war-torn, bloodied planet today, the spacemen ask. As I would inquire into the kind of "government" that would be implemented aboard the International Space Station, the answer always came back, "a corporate-styled" or "maritime-fashioned" form of government. When probed deeper on the subject, it became clear that they had more in mind a "global" view rather than a "naval" or military-styled system.

"What kind of economic system would be established in this terrestrial community?" I would ask. "Well, naturally, a *cashless, digitized* system is the only system that could work. Whose single currency could we recognize that would be acceptable to all aboard? It would have to be an electronic currency for such an advanced system as we would have. It would be our ultimate hope that ours would be seen as a workable model for the nations of the earth at large."

I remember a comment made by a Canadian space consultant at a banquet one evening. A number of international executives were seated at our table. As we began talking in *global village* overtones this Canadian specialist said, "Quite frankly, my friend, speaking just for myself here at this table tonight, I can honestly say that I no longer see myself as a Canadian. In fact — professionally speaking — I always present myself as a Global Citizen! Since I have established residences in more than one country through my international travels, I think it's silly to identify myself with any one country, don't you?" As I looked around the table, I saw a number of executive heads nodding in agreement with his position.

The man then proceeded to pass his business card around the table, on which he had his three or four office locations (in as many countries), showing his title as Global Space Consultant. Four different international phone numbers with the *world* as his office! I think he successfully convinced the other execs around the table that night to get their business cards changed in like manner.

"The nation-states are through!"

American futurist Hazel Henderson, in July 1980, declared before the First Global Conference on the Future in Toronto, Canada: "This new world order is inevitable, even if the keepers of the old order resort to violence to try to stem the tide. The competitive, aggressive, patriarchal, machismo nation-states are through!"

Indeed, the end of "nation-states" has long been both the fantasy and target of political pundits and corporate researchers for the past quarter century or more. World economist and business strategist Kenichi Ohmae, in his 1995 book, THE END OF THE NATION STATE, observes how the growth of global communication technology has altered the face of the world just in time for the onset of the next millennium.

Among the driving forces of the coming new era of global business, Ohmae notes, are the "irreversible" effects of technology — in particular, modern information technology — on the structure of business processes and on the values, judgments and preferences of citizens and consumers in all parts of the world. Indeed, so powerful are these effects that, once the genie of global information flow really gets out of the bottle — and it is certainly out of the bottle now — there can be no turning back. Against this kind of current, no traditional strategy, no familiar line of policy, and no entrenched form of organization can stand untouched or unchanged.

According to Ohmae, the idea of nation-states is so antiquated and slow in responding to the high speeds of global information technology, that the question begs to be asked if they are now worth preserving.

"In today's more competitive world," Ohmae writes, "nation-states no longer possess the seemingly bottomless well of resources from which they used to draw with impunity to fund their ambitions. These days, even they have to look for assistance to the global economy and make the changes at home needed to invite it in.

"Are nation-states really the primary actors in today's global economy?" he asks. "Do they provide the best port of access to it? In a world where economic borders are progressively disappearing, are their arbitrary, historically accidental boundaries genuinely meaningful in economic terms? And, if not, what kinds of boundaries do make sense?"

I realize that, when we opened this chapter, we started discussing an *evolving* information system, but we also opened with a question — "evolving *toward what?*" In case you missed it, what is fueling this birthing of a new global society is *the technology* — in particular, global communications technology as it affects and alters everything it touches. Despite ourselves, the world is going global!

National Editor for *Rolling Stone* magazine, William Greider, has written a book with an intriguing title: ONE WORLD, READY OR NOT! "The diversity of the world's peoples is converging in this common experience: the delight of encountering new inventions, magical gadgets or electronic machines that seem smarter than people," he writes.

"The symptoms of upheaval can be found most anywhere," he continues, "since people in distant places are now connected by powerful strands of the same marketplace. The convergence has no fixed center, no reliable boundaries or settled outcomes. As enterprise opens up new territories, the maps keep changing — changing so rapidly that is has already become common-place to speak of *one world* markets for everything from cars to capital. The earth's diverse societies are being rearranged and united in complicated ways by global capitalism. The idea evokes benumbed resignation among many. The complexity of it overwhelms. The enormity makes people feel small and helpless."

Not only does the Internet and its sundry peripheral systems want to grow to encompass the entire planet, but the greater question beckons: What will be the *end result* of such a growth? As a society, we eagerly buy the latest toys of the current *InfoTech* revolution, but what are we buying into? As we proceed with this treatise, the answer will become increasingly clear. It may not be what we bargained for as we clip yet another communication device to our belt or slip another plastic card into our wallet.

- - - - - - - - - - - - - - - - - - -

"It is possible that after a few decades of global communications, <u>civilizations</u> will become *worldwide threads.* New global influences will grow up.

"Patriotism is declining and may decline more with decades of advanced global communications. Some people will feel more loyalty to their global cultural thread than to their country. An English computer specialist with IBM feels more in common with a Japanese IBMer than with an English poet. American and Russian astronauts together exhibit understanding and loyalty that transcends national differences.

"Some Europeans now claim to be Europeans first and Germans or Belgians second. We hear corporate executives make statements such as 'We do not think of ourselves as a Dutch company, but as an international company with a head office in Holland.'

"In ancient Greece, there were city-states. Later, there were nation-states, which merged into larger groupings. A pattern of the satellite age may be something rather like *corporation-states*, employing hundreds of thousands of people worldwide, linked together by global video, voice, and data links, moving funds around the world electronically."

— James Martin
TELEMATIC SOCIETY

Chapter Two

The *Invisible* Internet

"The Internet is a global network of networks, enabling computers of all kinds to directly and transparently communicate and share services throughout much of the world. Because the Internet is an enormously valuable and diverse tool, enabling the capability for so many people and organizations to communicate and interact, it also constitutes a shared global resource of information, knowledge and means of collaboration and cooperation among countless diverse communities."

That's the definition of the Internet that is put forth by The Internet Society on their website, *http://www.isoc.org/internet*. Indeed, the Net is truly a researcher's heaven, but it can also prove to be a parent's worst nightmare in terms of monitoring and screening what their children have access to.

The Internet has grown so far so fast in such a short period of time, it's being called the *fastest* growing technology in the history of man. At the Old Executive Office Building in Washington, on November 30, 1998, Vice President Al Gore hosted a mini-seminar into the future of the Internet and the Information Superhighway. Present at the one-day workshop was a consortium of White House staffers, members of Congress, state government officials and department heads, a contingency of corporate business leaders and the President himself. The Vice President made these observations concerning the World Wide Web:

"With 140 million users now around the world and 52,000 more Americans logging on for the first time every single day, the Internet is remaking the way we live, the way we learn, the way we work. More messages are now sent by e-mail than by regular mail. And, what began as a specialized network for computer scientists, has become a global nervous system for the entire world."

Then, Mr. Gore mentioned one of the expansion ports for a *newer*, enhanced Internet of the future. "The Global Information

Infrastructure, or GII, a *network of networks* that sends messages and images at the speed of light on every continent — this would help us build *a true global electronic village* to expand access to all forms of communications."

In closing his comments at the meeting, Mr. Gore capped it all by saying, "The simple fact is that, in today's global economy, we are all connected. *Global interdependence is not a policy; it is a reality!*"

The issue of *global interdependence* upon the computer and its resultant interlinked communications system — its "network of networks," as Mr. Gore identified it — presents an ominous side that is difficult to ignore, despite its glowing accomplishments.

"All modes of communications we humans have devised since the beginnings of our humanity are coming together now into a single electronic system, driven by computers," writes John Wicklein in ELECTRONIC NIGHTMARE: *The New Communications and Freedom.* "Although this new communications system will bring us many benefits, it will also put us in danger of losing our individual liberty."

"The computer has wrought a fundamental change in American life by encouraging the physical migration of information about the most minute details of our personal and public lives into the computerized files of a large and growing number of corporations, government bureaucracies, trade associations and other institutions," says David Burnham in THE RISE OF THE COMPUTER STATE. "In addition to allowing large organizations to collect large amounts of detailed information, computers and the *linked telecommunication networks* have considerably enlarged the ability of these organizations to track the daily activities of individual citizens."

Consequently, Burnham goes on to say, "telecommunications equipment and computers have tended to *centralize* the power held by the top officials in both government and private industry. Who controls what information is stored in the great data bases of the United States and who serves as the gatekeeper to most of the giant communication networks?"

It's this loss of personal privacy that makes the idea of a *disappearing, hidden* Internet all the more ominous.

"Today, we have at our disposal new machinery of great power," writes James Martin in TELEMATIC SOCIETY. "We can collect, transmit and analyze thousands of times the information we ever could before. The conflict between privacy and other social values suddenly becomes acute.

"One common concern about a telecommunications society is that computers could keep track of people. Today, many different machines contain many different pieces of information about us ... Electronics could make our lives as visible to officials as that of a goldfish in a bowl.

"What sort of current will be generated when the world's billions are suddenly wired together?"

These poignant questions and probing analyses of our times become more credible in light of current trends to take the Global Information Network to new levels. The Internet is about to go both underground and behind the walls of our daily existence. It's destined to become the ultimate Big Brother tool of Orwellian proportions!

TIME magazine, November 11, 1991, in its cover story entitled, "No Place To Hide," noted that "It may be customary to think of threats to privacy in Orwellian terms, with an all-seeing Big Brother government as the culprit. But lately the threat comes no less from private companies, private citizens — and from our own imperfect notions of how to define which matters are properly kept confidential.

"In the not-too-distant future, consumers face the prospect that a computer somewhere will compile records about every place they go and everything they purchase. Even government agencies are plugging into commercial databases to make decisions about eligibility for healthcare benefits and Social Security."

Progressive Grocer magazine of February 1997, raised the very same issue in its feature story, "Big Brother is Watching!": "Has technology brought us to the portal of a brave new world of telecommunications, or are we entering the dark place — an Orwellian society where *Big Brother* is watching us?"

"The Orwellian world of 1984, in which government controls the collection and dissemination of information and, thereby, controls much of what people know and think, is just around the corner," said Jerome S. Rubin, head of Mead Data Control in Ohio, in the April 24, 1978 issue of *ComputerWorld.*

In the world of total *ubiquity* (invisible omnipresence), such threats become very real ... and it's total ubiquity that is the next evolutionary step for the World Wide Web!

"Ubiquitous computing puts computing in the periphery of our lives, as a tool, not a focus," writes the students of the Computer Science Department at Virginia Tech, in their book, WORLD WIDE WEB: BEYOND THE BASICS.

"The term *ubiquitous* is used because computers and computation will be everywhere," they say. "Embedded in the fabric of our lives. It envisions appliances that can dial in and download or schedule repairs, control panels that know the location of your co-workers, or even clothes that know when they need to be washed ... Ubiquitous computing will bring the Internet into our daily lives with less effort."

The concept behind ubiquitous computing is to *hide*, or embed, computer technology into every thing we touch ... and everything that touches us. In doing so, the items that are so embedded become trackable and traceable.

"What this means is that (silicon, computer) chips are becoming cheap and tiny enough to slip into *every object we make*," writes *Wired* magazine's executive editor, Kevin Kelly, in his book, NEW RULES FOR THE NEW ECONOMY.

"Eventually, every can of soup will have a chip on its lid," Kelly writes. "Every light switch will contain a chip. Every book will have a chip embedded in its spine. Every shirt will have at least one chip sewn into its hem. Every item on a grocery shelf will have stuck to it, or embedded within itself, a button of silicon. There are 10 trillion objects manufactured in the world each year and the day will come when each one of them will carry a flake of silicon.

"If National Semiconductor gets its way, soon every FedEx package will be stamped with a disposable silicon flake that smartly tracks the contents of the package on its journey. And, if an ephemeral envelope can have a chip, so can your chair, each bag of candy, a new coat, a basketball. Soon, all manufactured objects, from sneakers to drill presses to lamp shades to cans of soda, will contain a tiny sliver of embedded thought."

The secret behind a ubiquitous communication system is in the nature of its viability — its ability to remain always open, ever *there* — its omnipresence!

"Today's consumer Internet is not what anyone wants. Users don't like it, ISPs (Internet Service Providers) don't like it, and phone companies don't like it," Tom Lyon, founder/chief technology officer for Ipsilon Networks, said in his keynote address at the Spring Network + Interop '97 trade show in Las Vegas in May, 1997. "For acceptable service and sustainable growth, we must abandon the dial-up model of Internet access. The Internet is moving too fast to be reinvented."

In other words, it's a matter of leaving the channel *open* all the time. No more dialing in to get a connection. The connection is never broken. It's never closed. Whatever the appliance or machine that is used for the connection to be complete, that channel is left always open between that entity and the Network Channel. It's an open protocol that is never closed.

Wired magazine, October 1996 edition, article: "The Embedded Inter-net," by David Kline, broadcast commentator for National Public Radio network: "The next big thing to hit the Net will be wiring together millions of tiny computers embedded into everything we use. This is no future vision; the products are hitting the market now!

"Today's personal computers and the Internet are at the stage where home motors and electricity were 100 years ago," he goes on to say. "They are poised to *shrink and disappear* — blending into the background of our daily lives."

David St. Charles, president/CEO of Integrated Systems, Inc.: "This is where we make the Internet real. And I mean, as ubiquitous as electric motors or telephones, where all sorts of devices easily and automatically communicate with each other with no one having to know anything about computers or software or TCP/IP stacks or anything else. *It's everywhere, it does everything,* and it's a no-brainer to use. *It's the pushbutton Internet!"*

Wired magazine once again, this time an article that appeared on the publication's website *(www.wired.com)* in January 1999 entitled, "Networking Everything," by Vince Beiser: "In the not-too-distant future, the Internet will link more than just computers. It will hook up everything from your toaster oven to your dog!"

"The Internet revolution has barely started," writes the renowned *father of ubiquitous computing* — Mark Weiser, chief technologist at Xerox Palo Alto Research Center (PARC). "(The revolution) won't be done until *everything* is on the Web. Light switches, pagers, copiers, printers, as well as PCs, benefit from Web connections ... Our computers should be like an invisible foundation that is quickly forgotten but always with us, and effortlessly used throughout our lives."

"Future access to the Web may not always be through desktop computers," the Computer Science Department at Virginia Tech writes. "Common equipment, such as telephones or even toasters, will connect to the Web, and the user may not even be aware of which appliances in the home are actually connected. Instead of the user taking the active role in connecting to the Internet, the user's tools will automatically connect, without the user's participation.

"The goal of ubiquitous computing," the authors go on to say, "is to move computers away from the central focus of the user's attention and into the invisible world, *where they are used subconsciously,* to enhance existing tools or communications."

"Today's *ubiquitous computer chip* is now being produced globally at the rate of nearly a billion per minute and is found in everything from super-computers to inexpensive children's toys," writes Vanderbilt University professor and former executive for Nortel and DuPont, Richard Oliver, in his book, THE SHAPE OF THINGS TO COME.

As noted earlier, Dr. Mark Weiser has written extensively on the subject of *ubiquitous computing* and the overall destiny of the Internet to go totally embedded.

From an article entitled, "The Coming Age of Calm Technology," dated October 5, 1996 (posted at Weiser's website:http://www.ubiq.com/hyper-text/weiser/acmfuture2endnote.htm), the *father of ubiquitous computing* introduces us to the concept that, to-date, our hi-tech world has already taken us through two and-a-half phases of computer evolution.

Phase One: *Mainframe Era*	Many people share one system
Phase Two: *PC Era*	One person to one computer
Transition	Between current Internet & Ubiquity
Phase Three: *Ubiquitous Computer Era(UCE)*	Many Computers share one person

"The Third Wave of Computing," Weiser writes, "is that of ubiquitous computing, whose crossover point with personal computing will be around 2005-2020. The *UC Era* will have <u>*lots of computers sharing each of us.*</u>"

This last statement is particularly disturbing because of its over-centralized, heavily bureaucratic, Big Brother implications. Just think for a moment what is being suggested here by "many computers *sharing* each of us"! What are all of these computers seeing? What are they saying to each other about us? What safeguards will there be against potential abuse?

Weiser goes on to describe how the ubiquitous computing (UC) of tomorrow will be "embedded in walls, chairs, clothing, light switches, cars — in everything. UC is fundamentally characterized by the connection of things in the world with computation. This will take place at many scales, *including the microscopic*."

The Internet that is coming will be far more complex than it is right now. With its continually open protocol, it promises to not only be the most interactive network ever conceived, but the most pervasive as well.

"UC will see the creation of *thin servers*," Weiser continues, "costing only tens of dollars or less, that put a <u>full Internet server into every household appliance and piece of office equipment</u>. The next generation Internet protocol, IPv6, can address more than a thousand devices for every atom on the earth's surface. We will need them all."

The goal here, according to Weiser, is to create a high tech environment that poses no threat to the human psyche ... a technology so user-friendly, so enmeshed into man's world so as not to be noticed ...that the *marriage* between man and machine would appear almost seamless. It's a phenomena that Weiser and others are calling "Calm Technology".

"If computers are everywhere, they better stay out of the way," Weiser writes, "and that means designing them so that the people being shared by the computers remain serene and in control. *Calmness* is a new challenge that UC brings to computing. When computers are used behind closed doors by experts, calmness is relevant to only a few. Computers for personal use have focused on the excitement of interaction.

"But, when computers are all around, so that we want to compute while doing something else and have more time to be more fully human, we must radically rethink the goals, context and technology of the computer and all the other technology crowding into our lives. *Calmness* is the fundamental challenge for all technological design for the next fifty years."

- -

"Eventually, every can of soup will have a chip on its lid. Every

light switch will contain a chip. Every book will have a chip embedded in its spine. Every shirt will have at least one chip sewn into its hem. Every item on a grocery shelf will have stuck to it, or embedded within itself, a button of silicon ... Soon, all manufactured objects, from sneakers to drill presses to lamp shades to cans of soda, will contain a tiny sliver of embedded thought."

— Kevin Kelly
New Rules for the New Economy

Chapter Three

The Loss of Privacy in an
Over-Networked World

"Today's *ubiquitous computer chip* is now being produced globally at the rate of nearly a billion per minute and is found in everything from super-computers to inexpensive children's toys," writes Vanderbilt University professor and former executive for Nortel and DuPont, Richard Oliver, in his book, THE SHAPE OF THINGS TO COME.

The globalization of the world through hi-tech, ubiquitous communications and the spin-off *bio-materials* (computer-aided technology ware such as clothing, shoes, appliances, etc.) will carry us down to the lowest degrees of human society, Oliver points out.

"For business, the energy of the Industrial Age, coupled with the global electronic embrace of the information hardware and software of the Information Age, has had the effect of abolishing the constraints of both time and space ... In many ways, then, the Industrial Age made us *one world*, the Information Age made us *one village*, and now bio-materials will make us *one family*."

The architects and designers of this ubiquitous communication system are serious in the system they are birthing. To read their materials is to come away persuaded that they actually DO believe in the mutual benefit of what they are creating. Nonetheless, the world they are helping to build (because of *marketplace competition)* can not guarantee that there won't someday, from somewhere, come those who will see and capitalize on the fullest ramifications for world control as one can imagine.

Once again, Jeremy Rubin as he was quoted in *ComputerWorld* magazine on April 24, 1978: "Besides the danger of an Orwellian society, there is another danger inherent in the collection, organization and dissemination of information by government: the government has difficulty regulating itself."

"Telecommunications equipment and computers have tended to *centralize the power* held by the top officials in both government and private industry," writes Burnham in THE RISE OF THE COMPUTER STATE. "In what ways does the computer enlarge the power of public and private organizations over the individual citizen? Computers have allowed far more organizations to have far more access to far more people at far less cost than ever was possible in the age of the manual file and the wizened file clerk."

What all this capability presents is the possibility for the extremes of human nature to run amok when presented with the *power of omnipresence!* Don't forget — history HAS presented its share of messiah-like leaders who didn't know when to stop in their pursuit of historical legacy.

Remember Mark Weiser's "many computers sharing one person" concept of the third phase — the *Ubiquitous Computing (UC)* era? Well, yet another author has played on that same theme. "Many different computers collect data about an individual," writes James Martin in TELEMATIC SOCIETY. "In total, the data they store could form a formidable and highly personal dossier if it were gathered together."

John Wicklein agrees: "Any one who runs a computerized, two-way (interactive) communication system has a magnificent tool with which to invade our privacy. This, in fact, is the most urgent area of concern in the development of the new communications — including computerized storage and electronic exchange of personal data collected by government agencies, credit rating concerns, personal investigation companies, and private employers.

"One of the great dangers to freedom posed by the new communications system lies in this area of computer-assembled dossiers. Since their inception, commercial and government computer data banks have out-distanced efforts by Congress and the public to regulate their use ... The invasion is well under way."

Two case histories will bear out the impact of this issue of "privacy lost" more clearly than anything else. Both cases are, by most standards, considered to be old and irrelevant ... but, in review, consider once again how far we have come technologically since the stories first ran, and see if you're not convinced that, indeed, these stories are as relevant today as they have ever been.

- - - - - - - - - - - -

From the *Houston Chronicle* of May 18, 1986 comes this item that ran originally in *The Washington Post*, entitled: "Big Brother Alive & Well in U.S. Maze of Computers."

John first spotted her on his way to work as they were both waiting at a traffic light. Everything about her was striking: mid-30s he guessed, chestnut hair, driving a steel blue Mercedes with vanity plates that read: MINE.

Upon his arrival at the office, he went immediately to his computer, pulled out his list of codes, and went straight to work. Tracking down this beauty would be a cinch, he thought, as he settled into his position as a social worker with numerous public and governmental records at his disposal. Checking out people had become such a natural part of what he does; it *was* his job.

First, he accessed the computerized records of the Department of Motor Vehicles. Typing in the letters "M-I-N-E," he sat back and waited. Sure enough, onto his screen, came the following:

License Tag:	*M I N E*
Vehicle:	*1984 Mercedes Benz 190E*
Owner:	*Marci Hamilton*
Address:	*2727 Skyline Drive*
Drivers' License No.:	*524646789*
Birthdate:	*090551*
Sex:	*Female*
Weight:	*105*
Height:	*5'6"*

Knowing that Marci's drivers' license number is the same as her social security number, it was an easy thing for him to gain additional information on her, such as her current financial record; where she worked; the names and ages of her two school-aged children and where they go to school; her marital status (divorced); the name and current work and financial record of her ex-husband; and much more.

John also learned that Marci owns a 25-foot sailboat valued at $15,000. Through her tax records, he reviewed her earned income, including that from various bank CDs, dividends from stock and savings interest, income from rental property, executive sales bonuses and some wagering at the local race track.

Having completed his own personal dossier on his prey-of-interest, John was finally ready to make his move. He chose to call Marci at work.

"Good afternoon, this is Ms. Hamilton," she answered. "I don't want to sound too forward," John began, "but I feel I already know you. You see, I met some people at a party the other night and they told me all about you and your little girl, Lynn — with the hearing problem — and how Andrew, I mean, *Andy*, is so smart in school."

"Really! Who told you about us?" Marci asked. "Well, this is really embarrassing, but I don't remember their names. It was a big party, you know. They said we had a lot in common — like, weekend sailing ..."

The second case history, reported in *The Guardian* newspaper of London in November 1980: "While training as a teacher in London, *Jane Smith* stayed for ten days in a licensed squatters' apartment. Two years later, she took an injured political demonstrator to a hospital. A year after that, police removed marijuana plants from the apartment she had stayed at three years earlier. At the same time as the marijuana discovery, a former boy-friend gave her name at a venereal disease clinic as one of his romantic, intimate contacts. Because of the breakdown of their relationship, Jane had become depressed for which her doctor had prescribed anti-depressants." This story appeared in an article entitled, "The Computer Watched Society."

So, consider the dossier that has been crafted by the computer database on her. According to the article: "Jane's computer dossier file reveals her to be an *ex-squatter, sexually promiscuous (with) criminal associates charged in drug trafficking; having (political) extremist connections; (and is) mentally unstable.*"

The article raises a question pursuant to a psychological profile on Ms. Smith relative to her chosen career, that of teaching. "Would you give a job or financial credit to Jane Smith?" the article asks. "Jane has applied for a teaching position, placing her in contact with children. Accordingly, she would very likely be turned down based on the dossier alone."

Question: Given YOUR basic, personal, private beliefs and social practices, *could this happen to you?* What would be your response if it did?

As society has become more dependant upon the fruits of advanced technology, that same society has also been more easily influenced, controlled, manipulated and anesthetized by those same fruits. We've also become more predictable, surveyable, observable. Consequently, we've been indexed and catalogued, qualified and clarified, verified and categorized, scrutinized and homogenized ... so that sterile observation may result in global quantification.

"The difficulty is that computers do not discriminate between socially useful information, like medical needs, and socially dubious data, like political beliefs," *The Guardian* article reports. "Perhaps the computer era's most striking element is that we are no longer citizens or individuals. Just as the industrial revolution led people to be defined as *hands*, the computer has redefined us as well. We are all, now, *data subjects.*"

The ever-growing and evolving Information Superhighway, which includes all that is both wired and wireless communication technology, has given rise to the most outstanding Big Brother system imaginable. Cradle-to-grave dossiers on multiplied millions of individuals world-wide is now the norm. Information networks now circle the globe speeding data from home to office, from office to headquarters, from headquarters to the classroom, from the classroom to the satellite, from the satellite to millions of linked conclaves below. Private networking eventually gives way to open inter-networking which, in turn, paves the way toward regional, national and global centralization.

Congressman Bob Wise (D-WVa), quoted in *TIME* magazine November 11, 1991, in a cover story article entitled, "No Place To Hide," said, "Privacy watchdogs are warning that the combination of invasive technologies and lax laws threatens to make the U.S. a nation of people who live in glass houses, their every move open to scrutiny by outsiders."

"The law right now does not look good for privacy plaintiffs," says Andrew McClurg, law professor for the University of Arkansas and author of a study into privacy issues in 1992.

Now, translate all this back into the "world of ubiquity." In the "old" world of computer databases and interlinked networks, information that was collected was information stored for requested use. In the forthcoming world of ubiquitous technology, all that now becomes *real time* matter — information that is readily available and accessible "as it happens"! The *electronic economy* thrives on it.

"Why should a phone company get paid only once a month when you use the phone every day?" asks Kelly in NEW RULES FOR THE NEW ECONOMY. "Instead, it will eventually bill for every call *as the call happens, in real time.* The flow of crackers off grocery shelves will be known by the cracker factory in real time. The weather in California will be instantly felt in the assembly lines of Ohio ... In the *network economy*, only signals in real time are truly meaningful.

"The Net is not just humans typing at one another on AOL," Kelly continues. "Rather, <u>the Net is the *total collective interaction* of a trillion objects and living beings, linked together through air and glass.</u> This is the Net that begets the network economy."

"Today, we are (building) networks with multiple paths like *spiderwebs* (ed.: an apt description of *the Net*) which interconnect computers and computer users. These networks are spreading worldwide ... powerful computers becoming as common as telephone sets. Large expensive computers will acquire extraordinary capabilities and will be accessible via networks," writes Martin in TELEMATIC SOCIETY.

- -

"The government has the technological capacity to impose total tyranny if a dictator ever came to power. There would be no place to hide. There would be no way to fight back because the most careful effort to combine together in resistance to the government, no matter how privately it was done, is within the reach of the government to know, such is the capacity of this technology."

— Senator Frank Church
late Senator (D) - Idaho
Houston Chronicle - August 18, 1975

Chapter Four

R&D for the U.C.E.
Research & Development for the
Ubiquitous Computing Era

The headlines tell it all: <u>Communications News</u>: *"The Next Big Thing"*; <u>NewMedia</u> magazine: *"Internet Appliances: The Next Big Thing"*; <u>BusinessWeek</u>: *"Beyond the PC"*; <u>Popular Mechanics</u>: *"The PC You Wear"*; <u>ABCNews. com</u>: *"PCs for the Dash"*; <u>The Industry Standard</u> magazine: *"Now, on Your Fridge: The Internet"*; <u>U.S. News & WorldReport</u>: *"Brave New Home"*; <u>Home Office Computing</u>: *"A Home With A Wiring Closet"*; <u>PC Magazine</u>: *"Networked Appliances"* ...

"The next big thing is the *online-ness* of the world," states David R. Gellerman, vice president of technology and corporate development at Hekimian Labs (*Communications News*, March 1999).

BusinessWeek magazine, in its cover story of March 8, 1999, looked at the new era "Beyond the P.C."

"We're entering the consumer era of computing," said Donald A. Norman of Nielsen Norman Group consultants in the article. "The products of the future will be for everyone."

"The hi-tech industry is on the cusp of a new era in computing," *BusinessWeek* said, "in which digital smarts won't be tied up in a mainframe, minicomputer or PC. Instead, computing will come in a vast array of devices aimed at practically every aspect of our daily lives. Unlike complex desktop PCs, these *information appliances* ... will be simple and convenient.

"By 2002, more information appliances will be sold to consumers than PCs."

Enough Computing to Spread Around

In other words, the personal computer will no longer be the centerpiece of computing. At best, it will become the new mainframe for all the computing that is being done, whether at home, at the office, at school, or on the road.

"Mundane products already found in many homes will also get far smarter. Cameras, TVs, cell phones, and cable boxes are going digital, making it far easier to add new features that let them take on jobs now done by the PC — including Internet access," *BusinessWeek* reports.

For example, iReady Corp. (www.ireadyco.com) has created something they call "Internet-on-a-chip" technology that enables such things as TVs, fax machines, copiers and regular household appliances to be linked to the Internet for $10 or less.

"Low-cost but powerful computer chips will play a key role in the migration of Internet access capabilities to electronic devices other than personal computers," reported Inter@ctive Week on February 9, 1998, as it announced the debut of the new technology.

"The basic components of computing — processors, memory, storage, networking — are becoming so small, powerful, and inexpensive that, soon, computing will be embedded in all kinds of everyday things that don't look at all like computing devices: cars, roads, machine tools, vending machines, houses," writes IBM CEO Lou Gerstner in his company's 1998 Annual Report.

"When all these are connected to the Net," he continued, "they will make possible a new class of applications, invisible to end-users but vitally important to businesses and institutions.

"As the Net takes over much of the work previously performed by PCs, we're seeing another interesting development," he writes, "a proliferation of new personal computing devices, personal digital assistants, Web-enabled TVs, screen phones, smart cards, and a host of products we have yet to imagine."

Mega-Partnerships Guaranty Diversity and Progress

Around the world, mega-mergers and contract agreements are taking place throughout the hi-tech industry between giants and small players as the industry at-large prepares for the new era.

IBM and Japan Sharp, for instance, have announced a cooperative agreement in which both companies will work together in the area of *pervasive computing* — "the concept of controlling automobiles, home appliances and other devices equipped with integrated circuits via a network," noted *Reuters* on March 24, 1999.

"Their partnership could lead to the joint development of such items as microwave ovens that could take in cooking recipes from the Internet through a home network," the report said.

Other partnerships include Sony and Matsushita Electric teaming with Microsoft, while others are linking with Sun Microsystems, IBM, and Hewlett-Packard.

Wired magazine, in its April 7, 1999 online newsletter, carried a *Reuters* news story of still another alliance given to the future of ubiquitous computing, this one involving as many as "13 major computer, phone, and electric-utility companies." The alliance is called The Open Service Gateway Initiative (*U.S. News & World Report*, April 5, 1999; "Brave New Home").

"The group is designing a way to connect an array of devices — computers, telephones, appliances (like TVs, stereos and VCRs), along with security alarms and electric meters, and even refrigerators or toasters — to the Internet," the *Reuter's* report said.

"The alliance said in a statement that it wants to secure ways for Internet-based service businesses to deliver home services like security, energy management, emergency health care, and electronic commerce."

Major players in the alliance include Motorola, Lucent Technologies, Ericsson, Nortel, IBM, Oracle, Philips Electronics, Sun Microsystems and Enron's Communications unit.

In-Home Networking the Key

Already, the groundwork is being laid through the introduction of "home network" products that provide such things as wireless connectivity and compatibility between two or more home PCs to remote monitoring of appliances, property and environment from a different location via the Internet.

"Today, with the availability of high-speed modems and digital phone lines, crafty surveillance cameras and slick monitoring software, a number of manufacturers have developed complete remote monitoring systems made for easy set-up and installation," notes the December 1998 issue of *Electronic House* magazine. From one's own office or distant vacation spot, with little more than a laptop computer, today's tekkie-on-the-road can remain in constant, uninterrupted view of his home and property ... via the Internet!

Do you have a weekend get-away place down on the lake? Through the Internet, from your home or office, turn on the lights and the TV at the hideaway; adjust the air conditioning/heating; restart the hot water heater; re-establish phone service; and, during the winter months, clear snow off the driveway through specially placed heating coils that are tied into your home's electrical system — all courtesy of Internet-friendly networking software.

Mark Christensen, vice president and GM for Intel's Network Communications Group: "There's a fundamental change in the industry. There are more and more computers in homes and they are going to be connected."

Intel's *Anypoint Networking System*, for instance, allows the user to plug one end of the Anypoint box into a PC's printer port and the other end into a standard phone jack. From that point, the user identifies each machine that will be included into the host PC. As additional printers, fax machines and PCs are added in the future, Anypoint automatically configures them into the system. From here, family members can share files between PCs, individually surf the Web through the same host PC, or all play the same or different games through their individual stations.

"The next battlefield in computing will be over networking home appliances," says Pierre de Vries, Microsoft's Information Appliance division's director for long-term planning and design.

"We're going to a world where computing is something you encounter in all parts of our daily life and something you carry around with you during the day," he said in the April 5, 1999 issue of *U.S. News & World Report*, in an article entitled, "Brave New Home. "

"All sorts of things from toasters to TVs will be intelligent and hooked together," writes *PC Magazine* Editor-In-Chief, Michael Miller, in his March 9, 1999 editorial. "As we move to an era of distributed intelligence, where even lights have rudimentary two-way communication features, you'll see lots of new software, new hardware, and new processors."

"The new world of communications promises to change the landscape of society. It really is ushering in a new age," David Nagel, chief technology officer for AT&T, said in the April 5, 1999 edition of *Business Week.*

The revolution will be in the homes that are being built today for the future. The December 1998 issue of *Electronic House* magazine reported on "systems-built homes that are pre-wired for the future."

"The pre-installed cabling is comprised of four high-speed data lines (for phone, fax and modem) and a high-capacity coaxial (TV) cable. After the sections of the home are erected and the wiring within each section is connected, the home is ready for technologies like computer networking and whole-house video distribution."

Indeed, *Home Office Computing* magazine notes that home networking is now the hottest trend in home construction. "IBM wants you to buy a new house networked from the ground up — in *an intelligent community*," the April 1999 issue reported. "Intelligent communities linked by the Internet."

"Homeowners will log on to an intranet site to do business with a local merchant or conduct a PTA meeting, for example.

IBM is also exploring ways to network existing homes using noninvasive radio frequency (RF) wireless services and phone and AC power lines."

The *internetworked* home will be one in which every appliance, every switch, every plug is linked to the open protocol of the World Wide Web. In the following chapter, we take a closer look at the products, services and tools of a ubiquitous world.

"Some day, all of these devices will be connected to the Internet all the time. As Web developers, it's our job to figure out what the devices will look like — and what to do with them."

— Alan Zeichick
Guest Editor
WEBTechniques magazine
March 1999
"Home Page"

Chapter Five

The Products of Ubiquity

In the world of hi-tech, the general consensus is that an entire *generation* runs approximately three years. If true, then "a generation from now," according to *PBS Online*'s "Life on the Internet" series addressing the subject "Next Stop — the Future," the new technology that is coming "will become invisible. We won't even notice we are living life on the Internet."

"*Smart technology*, which allows machines to communicate not only with humans, but with other devices in order to keep a whole household running smoothly, is on the horizon," announced *ABCNews.com* on April 16, 1999 in a segment entitled, "Making Smart Tech Mainstream."

The laboratory for the lion-share of this embedded technology will, of course, be the home ... and, more specifically, *the kitchen!* And it's here — in the kitchen — that we begin our review of the *products of ubiquity*.

The Interactive Kitchen

As meal time approaches in the contemporary home of the 21st century (early — between 2000 and 2002), the "connected" kitchen is a haven of *living*, compatible, interactive appliances. **Dishwashers** that are in perfect balance with other machinery in the house relative to noise levels and energy usage. **Ovens** with built-in intelligence that allow for remote-control cooking programs and Internet-aided recipes tailored to you and your family's tastes.

The **refrigerator** has a Pentium II processor built inside and a "huge hard drive" that "packs more computing power than most PCs," reports *The Associate Press* on October 1, 1998. The fridge is made in Japan by V-Sync and is controlled by a touch panel monitor in the door and/or a built-in microphone.

The refrigerator's computing capacity is so large that the company even recommends the unit be used as the "command center" for all the other appliances of the house, such as the television sets, the central air conditioning system and the telephones.

Ron Strich, vice president of ICL, a British technology firm, says the *smart* refrigerator has the potential of being the most popular and efficient appliance in the whole house. "What's going to happen in the very near future is *packaging intelligence*," he was quoted as saying on *ABCNews.com*, dated April 15, 1999. "When I am low on milk, the milk carton itself will announce that I am almost empty and add itself to the shopping list."

In fact, the new *Screenfridge* (as it is called) "can be used to order groceries over the Web, read email, play games," or air your favorite TV show, *Wired* magazine reported on their April 7, 1999 web page. "Running low on ice cream?" the article asks. "No problem. Just swipe the near-empty bucket across your freezer's bar-code reader and a fresh supply will be on its way."

Containing a "standard modem," the Screenfridge also dons a 13-inch LCD touch-screen and a bar-code reader scanner built into its door. Once the shopping list is complete, it is then "beamed over the Internet to a grocer selected by the customer." As an added feature, you'll also be able to "dial in on the way home (to) find out if you're out of milk" at all ... so says an *AP* report dated March 15, 1999, announcing the partnership between Motorola and MIT Media Lab in the area of developing *smart* technology for tomorrow's homes.

Then there's the ***smart counter top***. Under-the-counter sensors are linked to a computer that is connected to the Internet. The sensors will read the UPC scanner tags of food product packaging. The computer will then, by way of the Web, guide you through a recipe. It also becomes a working inventory control system.

Not to be outdone, the ***microwave oven*** may become the most popular kitchen appliance yet for jobs beyond the two-hour roast. Enter the *Microwave Bank*, developed by NCR. It's a standard microwave oven with a standard computer keyboard on a hinge as a door.

From the April 7, 1999 online edition of *Wired* magazine, the Microwave Bank "is a standard microwave that can also be linked over the Internet to your bank account to pay bills, transfer money, and go grocery shopping on the Web. It works with touch-screen technology on the door, as well as voice recognition software."

On the matter of security concerning one's online banking experience via the microwave, the manufacturers have that covered as well, right there on your counter top. "NCR says that bank accounts could be protected by using voice recognition, iris scanning, fingerprint identification and password protection."

"It's how you can manage your finances in the room where you spend the most time," says Mark McCall, NCR spokesman. "You can multi-task to your heart's delight."

"Someday we are going to have little digital control threads running through the kitchen, so that appliances are intelligent enough to turn themselves on and off, not to mention coaching you through a recipe," MIT Media Lab's Mike Hawley was quoted as saying by *ABC News* on April 15, 1999.

Throughout the House

From front door to back door — and virtually every point in between — our homes are destined for the Internet. *Security systems* are now available that fully utilize the interactive accessibility of the Web so that, not only do the systems know whether or not you are at home, but *where* you are in the home. **Every room** in the house will monitor your presence through any number of biometric sensors and/or even closed circuit television or subscriber cable services.

And, now, with the recent invention of *Microwave Impulse Radar (MIR)*, every home in the very near future may contain its own radar system that can only promise to enhance home security systems all the more.

Discovered "by accident" by electrical engineer Tom McEwan as he worked in his garage on a "sophisticated diagnostic system for a laser at Lawrence Livermore National Laboratory," this "simple" radar promises to perform many tasks in the all-new telecommunication home. Within a very short time, writes Andrew Derrington in the *Financial Times* of London, "radar will be commonplace; every home will have a dozen sets."

These small and inexpensive ($10 to $15) systems will prevent your car from plowing through the back wall of the garage; gauge the level of water for your bath; and give rise to a whole new generation of radar-enabled toys and robotized home appliances. And, all it is, is a tiny device that currently fits on a 1.5-inch circuit board, with a destiny to be fitted onto a silicon chip.

Of course, one step beyond even this is the work being done on smart product applications at MIT's ***Digital DNA Lab***. "By wearing semiconductors embedded in our clothing *or even in our bodies* (emphasis added), computers could identify us and operate kitchen appliances, lights, heating and entertainment systems according to our preferences," says MIT Professor Neil Gershenfeld in the March 16, 1999 edition of *The Boston Herald*.

Motorola has partnered with MIT in developing what it calls *DNA of the digital kind*. "DigitalDNA combines the integration of our ideas and technologies with those of our customers to create everyday miracles," says Hector Ruiz, president of Motorola's Semiconductor Products Sector. "We are poised to show the world how DigitalDNA breathes life into innovations that already touch every aspect of our lives. We will exceed consumer expectations for the Digital Age by delivering what they've imagined," he said.

"***Clothing*** with computerized labels that can tell a washing machine which cycle to use ... a ***home entertainment center*** with *talking* components would free users from having to struggle with several different remote controls or download each machine's specifications into a universal remote," reports the *Associated Press* in its announcement on March 15, 1999 of the Motorola/MIT deal.

"***Doors*** that recognize and open for specific people ... (for instance) as it sees you coming with a load of groceries ... ***thermostats*** that respond to voice commands ... and a refrigerator that will read the bar codes of the products inside, so you can dial in on the way home and find out if you're out of milk," the report noted.

Meanwhile, in your chest-of-drawers are pairs of ***smart underwear*** that contain thermostat-controlling sensors "that wirelessly control the air conditioning" in a room (*ABC News'* Century.com website).

Are you in a room with others and they, too, are wearing smart underwear? No problem, because MIT's ***smart rooms*** will read the average temperature preference for each individual and either (1) maintain a comfortable average for everyone, or (2) where there is more than one AC unit available, maintain a mean average per room or section of a room into which all who prefer the same average can be gathered.

"Smart rooms track what you are doing, and could function like *virtual butlers* by sensing when you are ready to get out of bed and starting the coffee," reports *ABC News*.

In the ***Family Room***, of course, you'll find the brains — or central nervous system — to the domicile connection. All of the changes now taking place involving the television set, for instance, are too myriad to mention here, but, suffice it to say, the family TV set has long been the target for linking Everyhome in Everycity to Computers Everywhere (borrowing from Winn Schwartau's style in *Information Warfare*).

Advancements provided by such companies as AtHome (the cable-modem service), Microsoft's WebTV and US West's AtTV are enabling today's new TV sets to become the conduits for the Everyhome entry onto the Information Super Highway. Through these and other services, specially equipped television sets can now receive and send email, place and answer telephone calls, and surf the Web — all by way of a hands-free speaker phone ... without the need to purchase or learn a PC.

The intensity of such advancements only promises to heighten as time goes along, too. The Advanced TV Enhancement Forum is a coalition between industry heavy-hitters Microsoft, Intel, Disney, DirectTV, CNN and others representing both media and technology. As noted by FCC Chairman William E. Kennard in remarks he made before the International Radio and Television Society in New York City on September 15, 1998, in this forum is found "a computer software firm, a hardware firm, a studio, a satellite video provider, and a cable programming network — all coming together to make digital work for the marketplace ... *Digital* IS the future of TV. The transition to digital TV is inevitable!"

The Chairman went on to declare that this revolution is not for TV only ... but for *everything ... all around us ... throughout society!* "The fact is," he said, "entertainment and other content are becoming more digital every day. All segments of the global communications industry are going digital. Digitization is here. It's inevitable. It will change our lives."

The Smart Bathroom

In the ***medicine cabinet***, you'll have *smart pads* and *smart bandages* "fitted with sensors that detect and monitor a range of clinical factors, including the rate of healing or whether a wound has become infected," *Wired* magazine reported on April 17, 1999.

These smart bandages will also be able to "perform tests that today require laboratory analysis," the report said. They will, eventually, "dispense drugs or pain-killers according to the state of the injury," according to Edward Sternberg, president of BioKey, the company in Milwaukee with the patent behind this technology.

Additionally, according to ABC News of Thursday, July 22, 1999, the smart medicine cabinet will also know you personally by way of certain biometric identifiers, such as your fingerprints on the door handle to the cabinet, and iris scan and thermagram facial prints via a small camera located in the cabinet.

By way of the Internet, the smart medicine cabinet will know your prescription from your doctor, which medicine in the cabinet truly belongs to you, and how much dosage you are supposed to take and how much you have taken. It will even reorder your prescription for you when the time comes — all by way of its Internet connection.

Of course, you can't have a smart bathroom without certain other amenities of that environment being part of the revolution. For instance, as you stand before the bathroom's **smart mirror**, you'll be brought up-to-date on the morning news, current stock prices, and the local weather. The mirror will also let you view current traffic conditions off the Net.

And, then, there's the toilet ... the **smart toilet**, that is. Quoting the May 31, 1999 issue of *Newsweek* in its Special Report entitled: "Technology: What You'll Want Next" — the smart toilets "sensors analyze your output, and ship the data via Internet to health-care providers."

The data from the toilet's analysis is sent into your doctor's electronic archive files at his office. Now, if you're in a traffic accident or some kind of threatening situation involving your health, all paramedics would have to do would be to scan your national health smart card, or your federal I.D. card, or your new state drivers' license, and the latest health check information is immediately available ... updated in the most recent hour by your toilet.

But, what if the last time you "went," you weren't in your home bathroom. What if you were in a public restroom?

No problem here either. Are you wearing your *smart underwear*? Do you have your drivers' license on you at the time? Or, how about Philips' new **hot badge**, or the **active badge** from Olivetti Research Labs in Italy? Any one of these items are designed to transmit data via room and appliance sensors and scanners, identifying the wearer by name and other pertinent information. If you have any one of these devices or a combination thereof, public smart toilets will still be able to identify user with the data.

This way, not only will your doctor be able to keep tabs on your general well-being, but so, too, will your insurance companies, your employer, state traffic officials and just about any other agency, company or interested entity (ie: school officials, the courts, law enforcement, etc.) you can imagine.

Will even this technology be accessible over the Internet — to distant doctors in remote locations who would be able to read the diagnostic laboratory findings of a band-aid patch?

Listen to Alan Zeichick in his editorial that appeared in the March 1999 edition of *WEBTechniques* magazine, in an article entitled, "For Every Light Bulb an IP Address?"

"Imagine that *everything* is connected to the Internet. All the time. Every kitchen appliance, every automobile, every stereo receiver, every smart card, *every pacemaker*, every telephone, every light bulb. Forget about Web browsers. With that type of infrastructure, with every light bulb (well, probably, every light *fixture*) having its own IP address, what might one achieve?

"A **light fixture** could send a trigger to a home-maintenance system letting it know that the filament has burned out. A *security system* could ask a light to turn itself off. *Sensors on your body* could let the house know *where you are*, so the right lights would turn on to your preferred brightness level. If you doze off, lights dim automatically, your phone's ringer turns off, and the stove lowers the heat on the pot roast."

The *Associated Press* on March 15, 1999, agreed: "*Smart* technology, which lets machines communicate not only with humans but with other devices to keep a whole household running smoothly, is on the horizon."

"The next revolution in technology isn't for the hackers and the geeks," reports *Newsweek*, May 31, 1999. "It's more likely to rise up in the rinse cycle of Internet dishwashers, to heat up in connected coffee makers, to accelerate in the Web-surfing family sedan and to stare back at you from your biometric bathroom mirror ... Everything connected to the Net."

Beyond the Home

Returning to Zeichick in *WEBTechniques*: "If you wear a ***pacemaker***, your doctor's office could monitor its performance, as well as your overall health. When you enter a building, the building's systems could note the presence of the pacemaker, query a medical server to determine if any devices might cause any risk, warn you about their presence, and also alert any devices that might cause interference to turn off if you wander too close."

In the meantime, it's late at night and you want a ***cold soft drink.*** The problem is, you don't want to go to the corner mini-mart; their prices are too high. And, after all, you don't have that much change in your pocket. But, you'd sure like a cold one for no more than, say, 65 cents. A soda machine it is, but where is the nearest one? According to Zeichick, check the Net.

"If you wanted a Dr. Pepper, you could easily find out the location of the nearest machine containing that beverage," he says. "If you take the next-to-last can, the machine would alert the just-in-time delivery truck."

In an article titled, "America Online's First Wish" in the same March 1999 edition of *WEBTechniques*, editorial director Dale Dougherty tells more about the ***ubiquitous soda machine.***

"Since 1984, computer science students have been connecting unusual items such as Coke machines to the Internet. *Yahoo!* now has a category called "Interesting Devices Connected to the Net." You can use your Web browser to access these devices — for example, to check the temperature of soda cans in a Midwest college dormitory. You can see when the doorbell was last rung, and even turn on the ceiling fan in *Mike and Anthony's Wired Room* at Dakota State University.

"What makes these experiments interesting is not just the display of data but the ability to interact with devices over the Web. The Web can serve as a generalized communications interface to a device you never have to touch physically," he writes.

Big Boys Want to Play, too!

We mentioned this earlier — the idea of some of the world's biggest, richest, most entrenched heavy hi-tech hitters getting onboard the Ubiquity Train. Numerous mergers and partnerships in this field have been forged bringing together the unlikeliest alliances imaginable.

Numbered among them is America OnLine (AOL) which, in the second quarter of 1999, announced its intention of jumping into the ubiquity fray.

According to C-NET News.com on April 19, 1999, AOL announced plans to "offer services to small gadgets that connect to the Internet, eliminating the need for personal computers," the end result being more "computer-phobic customers" worldwide would be brought into the connected world.

"You really are going to have to appeal to a mainstream population," notes industry analyst Phil Leigh. And, this mainstream population is made up of what Leigh calls *computer-phobic people.* "These people are likely to respond to something that looks (more) like a telephone instead of a computer," he said.

CNET reports that AOL's decision to go this direction "comes at a time when major Internet players have become aware that these browser-enabled hand-held devices and set-top boxes are on the *verge* of taking off." One analyst for the research firm Jupiter Communications even went so far to say that we are going to "see a number of Web players rolling out new strategies for these devices, because otherwise they fear that they will be left behind."

It's a mad rush to the Finished Line to see who can corner the largest piece of the "Ubiquity Market" as possible. Such is the intensity of this new trend that it prompted technology specialist Daniel Biby, an expert in the field of Electronic Data Interchange (EDI), to write the book *E-D-I or D-I-E*, in which he made this observation of the near future: "By the end of this decade, companies that are not using EDI to transact business may have to face the consequence of *not doing business at all.*"

"I think it reflects an underlying trend toward *network ubiquity*," Leigh went on to say. "Connect *anywhere, anytime!* That is where we are heading," he concludes.

- -

"With the Web, we can get to information anywhere, no matter what machine we're using. We don't have to install special software. Now, there are efforts to make devices as machine independent as possible."

— Dale Dougherty
Editorial Director
WEBTechniques magazine
March, 1999 "The Last Page"

Chapter Six

"We Saw What You Did, We Heard What You Said, and We Know Where you Live!"

"In the age of information technology, the incentive to discard information has essentially disappeared. Since it's easy and inexpensive to store data in electronic form, management often decides to keep information for unspecified periods of time on the off chance that it might be useful in the future. In other words, today's default position is to keep data indefinitely."

— *Dr. Deborah G. Johnson*
Beyond Computing magazine
"Should Companies Hold on to
Personal Data?"
March 1999

In the supercharged world of *data mining*, the issue of "data usage" might be similar to that of the "invasion of privacy" (discussed in Chapter 3), but, in another sense, there is a difference between the two. The invasion of privacy may mean little more than the mere storing of the information gleaned and its use may be relegated to very restricted venues. At the opposite end of that same spectrum, however, lies the extreme opportunism found in what we would call *Big Brotherism* — the idea that any authority would choose to abuse its power over the usage of the information it possesses.

This is where the promises of calm technology run the risk of falling into bad times. Historically, the *more* information that can be gathered, the greater the opportunity for tyranny and despotism to rule. On this one note alone, dictatorships tend to overpower democracies.

"There has been growing concern that the ability for U.S. citizens to get a fresh start is disappearing," Dr. Johnson writes, who is a philosophy professor for the School of Public Policy at the Georgia Institute of Technology in Atlanta. "Records are now created with every move we make: buying merchandise with a credit card, seeing a doctor, making a phone call, even paying a toll on the highway with an E-ZPass.

"In addition, it is now much easier for companies to mix and match information from different databases and to analyze information with data mining tools (automated techniques to identify patterns and relationships in data).

"This combined information, along with newly discovered patterns and relationships, can then be used to create a profile of an individual and to make inferences about that person," Johnson writes.

Remember our two stories in Chapter 3 concerning John's pursuit of Marci by way of her license plate, and Jane's being denied a teaching position in England based on disjointed information compiled within her computer dossier? These are the risks Dr. Johnson is referring to.

"We may not have Big Brother (yet), but we do have a situation that is ripe for abuse," she concludes.

The Deceptive Joys of Smarter Toys

The challenge facing all of civilization on this issue, as we see it, lies in the lure of advancing technology.

"Through the Net, we can now access and operate any computer-controlled device," noted the PBS program, "Life on the Internet: *The Invisible Net.*"

"The more that happens, the scientists say, the more we'll start to weave the Internet into the fabric of our lives. The Net will start to fade into the infrastructure and become ubiquitous — be everywhere and yet go unnoticed."

For example: "The explosion is seventeen minutes away," the magazine ad for Hewlett-Packard begins. "A gasket is about to blow.

"*Now imagine.* A chip in the engine alerts an electronic service that the driver signed up for when he bought the car. This service locates the nearest garage, books an appointment, provides directions to the driver, pushes his next business meeting back an hour and arranges for a rental car to meet him at the garage.

"But that's only the beginning," the ad goes on to say as it appeared in the April 19, 1999 edition of *ComputerWorld* magazine. "Meanwhile, the car manufacturer is notified of the gasket problem (it isn't the first time!). And, while the auto giant considers retooling the line, the service drafts a recall notice and engages the help of a PR firm.

"*Wow*. A lot is happening here. Car, gas station, rental-car company, auto giant are all **seamlessly linked to the Internet** (emphasis added here). Not as a collection of websites or in a battle for eyeballs. But as a catalyst for the service-based economy. *The next chapter of the Internet is about to be written*. And it will have nothing to do with you working the Web. Instead, the Internet will work for you."

As we proceed to present other elements of the all-encompassing Internet, may the reader keep in mind that, despite the spectacular advances in all this technology, the ultimate goal in it all — no matter how innocuous its appearance or its function — is *networking!* And networking is but another synonym for *tracking*.

The Connected Suburb of Networked Homes

"The Internet is going to play a more central role in people's lives. It's going to be important for people **in the home** to share that Internet access," said Michael Rubin, director and general manager of the Consumer Desktop Division of Compaq Computers in Houston, Texas, in the January 5, 1999 issue of *The Houston Chronicle*.

"Fundamentally, what we are doing is ringing in the new era of the *digitally networked home*, and ringing out the era of the stand-alone home PC," he said.

As noted earlier, big hi-tech players are enjoining themselves to smaller companies in alliances and arrangements that are propelling the ubiquitous computing (UC) era at warp speed into the near future.

For example, the June 1999 issue of *Electronic House* magazine featured in its cover story "Neighborhoods of the Future" the idea that "new homes (will be) linked by technology" — to one another!

"A new community springing up near the western foothills of Scottsdale, Arizona's McDowell Mountains is destined to change all" that we have come to know about community, neighborhood living. Rather than rushing home each day only to recluse ourselves behind the four walls of our private sanctums, "DC Ranch is rebuilding that old-fashioned community spirit one brick at a time."

In this concept community of 5,000 homes, where virtually every home sits on a cul-de-sac (thus limiting the number of houses per "block"), and each cul-de-sac features a "pocket park" and extended walking paths, each new home is wired for the future ... a technological future that *promises* the very best in amenities.

"It's what's buried beneath the hot desert soil and installed behind the stucco walls of every house that makes DC Ranch a truly connected community," *Electronic House* reports. Throughout the entire community, there are miles upon miles of fiber optic cable residing in underground conduits that end at every home's curbside. For a modest monthly fee, each homeowner pays for a package of "bundled telecommunity services" that include "117 channels of digital cable programming, a 256K modem connection for nearly instantaneous access to the global Internet and a community Intranet, plus a variety of advanced telephone services like Caller ID, voice messaging and call waiting."

The fiber bundle of services is further managed inside each house with a "Gateway Box" from US West. One of the intriguing features of the box is that, while the family is watching television or surfing the Web over their TV, should the phone ring, "the Gateway Box automatically pops the Caller ID information onto the TV screen."

Additionally, "families with home computers can access Ranch-Net, a custom-designed Intranet site loaded with information about DC Ranch events and activities."

Over RanchNet, neighbors have email access and personalized chat room opportunities to one another; they can be in contact with doctors at a nearby hospital via computer. They can make reservations at area restaurants or place grocery orders over the closed community Intranet ... or, parents can peek into the day care centers or school classrooms of their children and even get a sneak preview of their child's report card before its posted over the Net.

That's not all. Not only is there connection outside the home and between the homes, there's connection also within the homes by way of the HomeStar system from Lucent Technologies. "Every one of DC Ranch's seven homebuilders are mandated ... to install the HomeStar wiring network inside every home they build," the article reports. "Comprised of high-speed telephone, data and coaxial (entertainment) cabling, the HomeStar system links TVs, PCs and telephones *together*."

What this means is that, now, every appliance in a house can be linked to the central communication and computation system within that house. While a school report is being composed in a back bedroom over one PC, that same student can use that same system to simultaneously talk hands-free over the telephone *and* watch the same TV channel (or a different channel altogether) that is being viewed in the family room downstairs ... all by way of her desktop PC and monitor.

Peripherally, homeowners can also add-on such things as security systems, surveillance cameras and additional entertainment equipment. With these add-ons, mother could be balancing the family checkbook on the computer in her bedroom while viewing her sleeping child in the next bedroom in the upper corner of her monitor.

The problem, of course, is the hidden *networking* factor in all this. As good as it may sound, all of these perks are still part of a network ... an internal linking that can, whether overtly or covertly, become part of an external linking — and that external linking can just as easily go regional and global.

"The ability to establish a digital trail is unlike anything we've had so far in history," says Stanford University's law lecturer, Constance Bagley (*Business Week*, April 5, 1999; "Special Report: Privacy").

Not Just *Certain* Homes, but *All* Homes!

This revolution taking place in what we would call the *all-networked home* (internal, external and global) is so encompassing that strides have been made to also include *all* homes whose construction pre-dates the revolution itself — in other words, EVERY home EVERYwhere!

The *Home Phoneline Network* is a consortium of home product companies that are funding the development and distribution of "hardware and software to support speedy networking solutions that employ standard telephone cabling prevalent in all homes," reported *Electronic House* of October 1998.

"The Home Phoneline Networking Alliance (Home PNA) is leading the charge to bring Ethernet technology to the home," reported *InfoWorld* magazine, October 26, 1998.

"The group is backing a new technology that uses existing phone wires in a house to connect home PCs; this approach to networking could improve both performance and installation," *PC World* said in its October 1, 1998 issue.

"In the business world, the real power of the PC revolution was unleashed only when PCs were networked together," says Compaq Computer's Rod Schrock. "The goal of the HomePNA is to extend that revolution into the home."

Once the house is network-connected by way of telephone lines to the outside world, all of its interior activities and conversations are hackable and trackable!

"You already have *zero* privacy. Get over it!" — Scott G. McNealy, Sun Microsystems, Inc. CEO; *Business Week*, April 5, 1999; "Special Report: Privacy."

Connected Transportation Systems & Vehicles

Once you leave the inner sanctums of home or office, you needn't feel alone or isolated. For starters, your own car has onboard systems that keep you connected to the outside world.

"Your dashboard is a pop-up display that shimmers at the bottom of your windshield, discreetly projecting reams of data that appear, disappear and reconfigure at your command," writes Michael Krantz and his team of co-editors in TIME Digital's "Tomorrow's Gadgets" special report.

"It's not just oil pressure and m.p.h.," Krantz writes. "You can have your email read to you via a wireless link to the Net. You can query your GPS for directions, or ask it to scan the morning traffic and chart an optimal commuting route. You can check on the car's maintenance needs, make cell-phone calls, send faxes, order takeout and so on.

"*Your dashboard, like almost everything else in your wired life, has become a potent, networked tool*," he says (emphasis added).

Under this new momentum, the idea of our cars and trucks being tied to the Internet while in transit is not too far-fetched. Today, all across the nation, commuters can log onto the Net and receive real-time data on current freeway conditions, traffic speed, detours and alternate routes. As smart freeway technology meets smart car technology system architects promise commuters a more fun and interactive ride to their destination.

New systems for inside the car are now poised to become commonplace soon. The **Clarion PC** is one such system that not only controls the car's audio system, but "offers optional wireless email reception, GPS navigation and directions, and an address book," reports *ABCNews. com* on December 23, 1998. The onboard PC is voice activated so the driver need not take their attention away from the traffic or their hands off the wheel.

Superchip technology promises to diminish further the size and bulkiness of what could be called *PC presence* onboard. National Semiconductor announced in October 1998 its development of the **PC-on-a-chip** technology. Carrying the power and memory of a 386 and 486 computer, the *Superchip* will link the family car to GPS satellites, provide wireless connectivity to the Internet, download email, support voice recognition software that supports vocal email from the driver, hands-free mobile phone communications, two-way faxing, and much more.

CellPort Labs, Inc. of Boulder, Colorado, unveils on their website (www.cellport.com) their "C/P Connect On-Board Communications Server" which "turns a vehicle into a Node on the Internet; uses the existing Internet communication infrastructure; provides open architecture hardware and software solutions; and rapid and low cost application development" ... all for inside your car!

There's even been talk of installing **onboard electronic payment** and debit card transaction equipment, enabling commuters the opportunity to make direct EZPass payments electronically on the nation's toll roads from their cars while in transit.

Such super technology on wheels is changing every familiar facet of tomorrow's vehicles. For instance, "the days of car keys are numbered," wrote Linda Jackson for *Connected2 News*, an "electronic Telegraph" online publication out of London, on their February 25, 1999 webpage. "A keyless ignition system, operated by a credit card sized gadget which slip into your wallet," is on the way. Once the car owner's true identity has been logged into the car's computer memory, all the owner has to do is push the ignition button on the car's dashboard to start the engine.

"As soon as the (owner's) card touches the car door, radio signals are sent from hidden antennae in the bumper and door handles to the chip card. In return, this sends an identification code," unlocking the doors and releasing the vehicle to the control of the owner, the article said.

Aircraft industry **black box** technology is also being installed, further fine-tuning connectivity access — and potential remote control — of today's vehicles. The National Highway Traffic Safety Administration announced in May, 1998, its testing of an onboard system that would automatically call 911 emergency centers across the country when equipped vehicles were involved in crashes.

According to the *Associated Press* of May 11, 1998, "the box also transmits the severity of the crash and whether the auto was hit in the front, rear or side or rolled over." Once the link has been made with

911, "the car's cellular phone automatically establishes a phone channel with the sheriff's department so a dispatcher can ask occupants whether they are injured."

In some advanced systems, a signal is sent from auto to satellite if the airbags are deployed.

"The auto industry, which has already stuffed its cars with microprocessors, is now getting serious about putting the Net in the 'Vette," reported *Business Week* in its May 31, 1999 edition.

"Picture this: as your alternator gets ready to burn out, your car posts email to find the nearest service station that stocks replacement."

As beneficial as this technology is under these and other dangerous conditions, there is, sorry to say, another side — a **Big Brother** side — to it all .... all, of course, in the name of *public safety*, but Big Brother technology nonetheless.

"Every '96-and-later car is controlled by OBD-II regulations," reports *Hot Rod* magazine in its September 1996 article, "No Hot Rodding Allowed." OBD stands for *on-board diagnostics*, and today's automobiles are already covered by OBD-I and OBD-II regulations that dictate the kind of onboard computers and environmental equipment we're presently using.

OBD-III, however, will prove to be the infamous "fly in the ointment" if it ever becomes law.

"The vehicle computer monitors pretty much everything on the car that relates to emissions, which is to say, *everything!*" *Hot Rod* continues. "If you change wheel or tire size, theoretically, the OBD-II computer knows it and may signal a trouble code that will make the car fail a smog check."

If OBD-III becomes law, however, here's where Big Brother becomes an irritating passenger. "OBD-III is OBD-II with transmitters which tell roadside sensors that a car either has malfunctioning parts or has been modified."

Each car, it appears, "has its own fingerprint, of sorts ... The car sends a signal to the DMV or local smog cops that you're a vicious law-breaker, and the appropriate agency, in turn, sends a signal back to the car, shutting it down via electronic means. You're dead in the water and the government owns your life. The technology to allow this to happen is already a few years old."

What's this technology got to do with the *embedded Internet?* Everything! ALL of this technology has the built-in connectivity capability through such things as remote sensing, GPS tracking, radio frequency identification (RF/ID), electronic scanning, PC chipping, emissions monitoring, and much, much more.

On December 18, 1991, President Bush signed into law the Intermodel Surface Transportation Efficiency Act (ISTEA), providing federal funding to the states for the development of a highly sophisticated **traffic management system**. When completed, the hi-tech traffic control system promised to improve on traffic flow, travel safety and, ultimately, air quality in participating cities and regions.

In speaking before the Houston Forum on Intelligent Vehicle Highway Systems in May, 1993, then-General Manager of Houston's Metropolitan Transit System (Metro), Robert G. MacLennan, said, "We're adding modern technology to the equation" of overall traffic control. "We're talking about smart streets, smart intersections, smart freeways and transitways, smart cars, smart buses, and smart commuters."

The 20-year project, which will take in no less than 75 major metropolitan cities, is expected to cost in the area of $1.6 trillion — not counting new technology development and deployment by the auto industry itself.

"*Getting there* will be decidedly easier with the widespread use of Global Positioning (Satellite) Systems," remarks Mark David, former editor-in-chief for *Automatic ID News* in his March 1996 editorial.

"Smart maps will show travelers, boaters and hikers their exact position and direction," he wrote.

"The automated highway system is not a pipe dream," noted Mike Doble, one of Buick's technology managers, in the June 2, 1997 edition of *Newsweek*. "It's for real," he said. Returning for a moment to **IVHS technology** (Intelligent Vehicle Highway System, or smart streets), we're reminded of a personal experience we had while researching and reporting on Houston's computerized freeway system and their new TranStar Center traffic control headquarters in 1996.

While touring the all-new "Mission Control Center" for all the city's freeways, I noticed on the color-coded "big board" map that one particular driver had passed through the EZ Tag sensor zone going a bit faster than the posted limit, thus changing the color in that zone from green to red. I asked my engineer host what information he had on that driver.

After keying in some pertinent query, the screen revealed some vital information about the owner of the vehicle, including the driver's mobile cell phone, his home address, his work address, and more. "What can you do about this ... this guy is speeding," I inquired.

Referring back to the screen, my host said, "Well, we do have his mobile phone number. We could call him and tell him we know he's speeding and, if he doesn't get the speed down, we'll send him a traffic ticket in the mail. That might scare him a bit, but it could be done."

Is this all mere pie-in-the-sky dream factory-type stuff? "Houston has been and continues to be the model for the nation when it comes to a major project of this magnitude and dimension," TxDOT's Wayne Jones noted at the time of our published interview (*DBA Houston* magazine, June 1996; article: "High-Tech Makes Streets Smart").

And, it's only a matter of time, when the final insult could pounce on top of us ... when our *free*ways become *tax*ways or tolled highways. Already, the application is underway in some metropolitan Asian and European cities. Users of the "freeways" are electronically logged-in as they enter, scanned as they travel, and logged-out as they exit the freeway. At the end of the month, they are sent an itemized statement with bill attached, showing in detail their use of the system that month and how much they owe in taxes for that month.

Don't think for one moment it can't or won't happen here. Already, your car's presence is known the instant it enters the freeway lanes and traced until it leaves. With state governments being as cash poor as they presently claim to be, it's just a matter of time. That's all.

Tracking Collective Blips of Bits

Pardon me a moment as we take a short side trip off the main highway of our theme. In this tour we are taking into the not-too-distant-future, there's something I want you to see that, in its own way, will play a highly significant and influential role when the time comes. Right now, it is not fully enjoined to this highway of ubiquity we've been on, but construction is well under way and, someday soon, a long-anticipated connection will be made.

The exit sign we are taking is marked, "Mass Mapping." As a researcher and reporter into this kind of technology since the late '60s, I've been through this stretch of road and the small stops along the way quite a few times, and I've been watching this area expand and grow quite rapidly.

Again, just to remind you — much of what you are about to see is not yet linked to the Information Superhighway. *BUT*, in a very short while, all of the hi-tech back roads of experimental labs, field testings, limited public trials and debuts and the like will give rise to its own special link to not just the main highway of Web networking, but it will have its own special lanes given to the higher, faster speeds of ubiquity.

As we take the exit for this short side trip, let's set the tone for the evidences you're about to witness. One of our tour experts at this juncture is Mr. Simon Davies, from his 1996 book, MONITOR: EXTINGUISHING PRIVACY ON THE INFORMATION SUPER-HIGHWAY.

"We are no longer playing with gadgets or devices. We are dealing instead with a technological canopy ... an apocalyptic view of the future creates scant concern for most young people. It's no longer fashionable among intelligent folk to admit to being *scared* or even *concerned* about computers. Smart people embrace technology ... people of all ages feel no fear of technology. All around, there is an air of acceptance. Slowly, *we are being fused* with the technology. And, as we become fused with the technology, human identity becomes less distinct ... We are witnessing a process of *mass pacification* ...

"There is no Big Brother enforcing compliance with this New Order. People will happily surrender their most intimate data ... Big Brother entailed conflict, but ours is becoming a society based on *Harmony Ideology.*"

This is what we are finding down this side road, if you will — the increased phenomena of non-distinct human identity. It's the idea that, as high technology becomes increasingly interactive and invasive, the individually identifiable human being becomes a lessening factor in the decisions of the day.

Borrowing once again from an earlier quote by Winn Schwartau in his book, INFORMATION WARFARE: "Artificial intelligence systems will have to decide which information is relevant and which is irrelevant; more computers to decide which other computers are worth listening to. Human intervention, even in the decision-making process, will no longer be possible. We will have to trust that the cyberpriests develop artificial intelligence machines smart enough — *human* enough — to make decisions with which we are comfortable."

The individual identity factor gets bogged down in the endless streams of digital data — both information taken *about* us ("data mining") and that data taken *from* us ("body mapping" — the ability to digitize information yielded by our own bodies to technology either attached directly to our bodies or that which scans our bodies from a distance).

In August 1995, *Popular Science* magazine reported on the new **Image Verification System** developed by Kodak that utilized "highly compressed digital" imagery. "The data is carried on the magnetic strip of credit cards or printed as a bar code on checks," the report said. "It can also be stored in the processing chip of new smart cards.

"When a store clerk swipes the card or check through a reader, the information is decompressed and displayed in color on a cash register screen. The clerk completes the transaction *only* if the shopper resembles his or her mug shot."

A month later, in September 1995, *Popular Science* addressed the issue further by reporting on a "security system consisting of an infrared camera and a computer using the heat patterns emitted by facial blood vessels to identify people quickly and precisely.

"The system's camera takes a picture of the heat radiating from a person's face. The computer then compares this picture, called a **thermagram**, with an earlier image stored in its memory."

According to this and subsequent reports from other sources, facial thermagrams are not affected by changes in air temperatures, such as cold days versus hot days, nor are they influenced by changed facial expressions, plastic surgery or heavy makeup.

As this technology has improved over the years, it is now being used to "pin-point known criminals as they walk along in a crowd" in some metropolitan test cities like London.

From the BBC in London, Tuesday, October 13, 1998, comes word of **"The Mandrake Face Recognition System"** that searches for "target faces" in the streets of Newham, a borough of London.

"Newham has a network of 140 street cameras as well as 11 mobile camera units," the report said. "Images beamed into the council's security centre in East Ham (are) compared with a database of target faces supplied by police. The system can isolate the targets from the crowds of people appearing on CCTV (closed circuit television). When a match is made, the computer highlights the target and sounds an alarm. An operator then checks the image and decides if it is necessary to contact the police."

Officials have indicated that the Mandrake System has already proved useful in locating lost, runaway or kidnapped individuals.

Similar systems are in use in the states for such things as border patrol. In another case, the report states, "one state in the US is using a database of millions of pictures to check on people who may be entering into more than one marriage, and another state is checking for duplicate drivers' license applications."

The July 1995 issue of *Auto I.D. News* quoted Dave Evans, CEO for TRS Corp., in an article entitled, "A Defaced Face Can't Beat the Heat," as saying, "The applications for this technology are endless. We envision a day when consumers won't need cards at ATMs."

Well, that day finally dawned on Thursday, May 13, 1999, at a bank in Houston with "the nation's first ATM machines that grant access to customers by scanning their eyeballs instead of processing numeric codes," announced the *Houston Chronicle* on May 14.

Bank United was the first in the nation to introduce the Sensar Iris Identification System. "The system uses a video camera to zoom in on a person's eye, photograph the colored portion and translate the images into a computer bar code unique to that customer." Once the information is stored, "in less than five seconds, a customer can withdraw cash, deposit checks and verify an account balance just by looking into a camera."

In light of this kind of data capture, can it be long before such data is both mined and networked? Why, the convenience-hungry public will demand it. After all, what benefit is it if such data is stored with just your bank alone? What about the grocery store, the service station, and the airline counter? These, too, are areas prone to long lines and patience-testing tempers as we wait either for ourselves or others to produce adequate identification.

But, that's not all. If you travel in and out of our nation's airports, bus and train terminals, then you know the hassles and headaches brought on by long lines gathered at the high-security checkpoints. Oh, the precious moments spent in emptying pockets, placing purses and travel luggage on conveyor belts, the sound of the dreaded "beep" which can only mean one thing — more precious time waiting.

Since mid- to late-'98, ports of travel have been experimenting with something called **"the body imaging machine"** which, if accepted, may very well deliver on its promise to shorten security gate clearances. The only catch is, these machines *literally* (in a photographic kind of way) "strip" you of your most sensitive privacy. You might call it: the electronic strip search.

The machine was first demonstrated on network television in late 1998, then profiled once again by the *Associated Press* on March 12, 1999 and carried in newspapers across the nation. By way of low-radiation imaging, the machine "looks through clothing," leaving the individual *virtually* naked to viewing security personnel.

As was originally demonstrated on ABC's *"Good Morning, America!"* in late-'98, the company executive who volunteered himself to be so viewed by the body imaging machine was viewed from the backside only. The low radiation image produced accurate skin tone coloring and complete nudity. Even his body hair was plain to see by the viewing audience, so excellent was the detail.

Such imagery technology photographs individuals from all sides as they pass through the scanning field. Anything placed within their clothing, attached to their bodies, or swallowed into their bodies (where this low radiation screening is teamed with organ viewing x-ray, microwave or ultrasound), will be made visible to viewers.

Mass Mapping involves, once again, a *common* practice of gathering reams of information on hoards of people all at the same time — one at a time — as individual "units" pass through the information-gathering spectrum.

For example, *Popular Science* (April 1997) reported on "The Suitcase Scanner." Utilizing the techniques provided by Magnetic Resonance Imaging (MRI) technology as is found and used in hospitals everywhere, airports are able to "screen luggage for explosives and drugs."

Using a variant level of MRI called **Quadrupole Resonance Analysis**, "a transmitter beams low-frequency radio waves at luggage, momentarily disturbing the alignment of the nuclei inside. As the nuclei realign themselves, they emit signals that are instantly analyzed by the system's computer. Each type of material emits a unique signal, making it easy to spot," in this case, "any explosives or illegal drugs."

Being that this is borrowed from MRI technology at today's well-equipped hospitals, and given that this kind of imaging activates a kind of signal "unique" in frequency to the item being targeted, is it too far-fetched to imagine that, likewise, the human body would react in the same manner as luggage, drugs and explosives? If not, then a multiplicity of human bodies can be scanned by this MRI/QRA at any given time or juncture, receiving in return individualized signals that can be logged into a memory-driven program for future reference and use.

The range of thermagrams may also be extended to beyond a mere four feet to that of, say, a police officer's powerful flashlight or car-mounted high-beam hand light, given the development by Georgia Tech scientists of ***the radar flashlight***. According to the January 1998 issue of *Popular Science*, the new flashlight will even see through walls.

"The flashlight actually uses radar rather than a beam of light to sense the presence of a person behind a wall or hidden in a room. The device projects a narrow beam strong enough to detect a person standing 4 feet behind an 8-inch block wall," the report says.

Additionally, "the radar flashlight is as sensitive as it is strong. Standing still will do no good against it, because what the flashlight actually detects is the minute movement of the body caused by respiration." The principal research scientist on the project is quoted as saying that "the radar flashlight requires a body movement of only a few millimeters to detect human presence."

Work is also being done by the same group of scientists to take the radar flashlight technology and develop it further to detect an "individual's radar heartbeat" (suspected as being unique to each individual) at distances ranging to 30 meters (approx. 96 ft.).

Can this technology be used over a distance? Well, yes it can. As we have seen thus far, the high-tech industry is talking of the day when you and I would be able to unlock and open doors by nothing other than our brain waves. Our home security systems will be able to read our ***biometric*** *signals* as they are easily translated by such technology.

In fact, one of the *fastest growing* technologies in this area of human tracking is "biometrics" — the science of using a body's own unique elements as viable identifiers. Fingerprints, voice patterns, heat emissions, retinology, and other strange sounding physics from within, all make up the science of biometrics and its interests.

Neuscience, a biolab company, introduced in May 1999, a personal identifier card called *Veincheck* which, according to *Auto I.D. News* of that month, "identifies people by the vein pattern on the back of their hand." The company is "marketing the technology with smart cards for user ID for PC-based access control, time and attendance and ATM solutions."

Marc Weiser and Roy Want, both of Xerox's Palo Alto Research Center (PARC), have been developing something called ***the active badge***. As Want points out, "the active badge is a small, people-locating device that is monitored by an infrared system. If you're wearing a badge, your coworkers can simply look at their office computer screen and know where to find you. The badge is also *connected* (wirelessly) to the telephone system, which will re-route incoming calls with your own special ring to wherever you happen to be" within the building confines, he says in the PBS series on *"Life on the Internet."*

Weiser goes even further with this same "people finding" technology when he talks about something called, ***The Minder***. Weiser describes it in the PBS report as "a tiny, pocket-size computer that can not only *connect to the Internet*, but also beam information back and forth with other Minders."

Weiser predicts "this keychain-sized device, or something like it, will eventually be connected over the Net to a thousand computers just by walking down the street."

Once again, all of this technology can be miniaturized and made transmittable over any distance — and, coupled with active and passive technologies, can be effectively networked as well.

"The world will soon be a place where not just communications but also torrents of information will be available just about everywhere," reported the April 1999 special section to *Scientific American* magazine, "The Best Use of Space," in an article titled, "New Satellites For Personal Communications."

Satellites that track people are no longer reserved for enemies of the state," reports *Wired* magazine of January 14, 1999. "Global Positioning System technology is now being used to monitor convicted criminals on probation, parole, home detention, or work release. Satellite Monitoring and Remote Tracking system, or SMART, allows corrections officials to *watch an offender's every move*."

Of course, the use of this technology is not limited to law breakers. Ordinary citizens can also "enjoy" the benefits of never being lost. The May 16, 1996 *USA Today* reported that "by using a receiver as small as a cellular phone, *anyone* can get a precise fix on his location. It works night or day in any weather, *anywhere* in the world.

"If you want someone else to know where you are, GPS *can be combined* with communications equipment, from cellular phones to messaging systems."

The article went on to quote one GPS official as saying, "It has applications in virtually *any walk of life* you can think of." Jim White, of Magellan Systems Corp. , added further, "It's pretty incredible stuff. Here you have a 10-ounce piece of gear in your hand that's going to tell you where you are anywhere in the world."

"The possibilities are endless," noted a brochure distributed by Earthwatch, Inc. that was highlighted in the *New York Times* of February 10, 1997 in an article on the GPS satellite constellation. "Vacationers will plan exotic sailing cruises along foreign coasts. Small retail businesses will have a better understanding of demographics."

They Know What's in Your Pantry

It's on this latter point — of retail businesses benefitting from GPS tracking information — that we would draw your attention to yet another popular form of information gathering and how we, as a society, think nothing of its invasiveness and its potential for abuse. We're talking about your purchase preferences using what is called *loyalty cards* ... or "frequent shoppers' cards."

"Recent advances in computers have made possible *point-of-sale* data collection systems," writes Anne Wells Branscomb in her book, WHO OWNS INFORMATION?

In chapter one, there is the subsection titled, "The Threat to Privacy of Targeted Marketing," in which Branscomb introduces the reader to the electronic intentions of those frequent shoppers' cards. "Each checkout counter holds a color computer screen and an electronic gadget to read the frequent shoppers cards the customers carry. Buried inside each plastic card is a computer chip that records every item purchased, along with the buyer's name, address, age, social security number, employer, income, debts, children, pets, and other personal information."

She goes on to call the cards "tools in a technological revolution changing the marketplace in a way that should stir fears that personal privacy is being invaded on a scale more massive than ever before."

With such cards, shoppers are granted (or led to believe they receive) additional, super discounts on specific items in the store. What the average customer doesn't realize, however, is what is being done every time that card is swiped.

Branscomb gives us a peek into the back office world of information miners: "Citicorp, for example, is building a National Household Purchase Data Base covering 40 million households — nearly half the homes in the United States — with information to be gathered from 12,000 retail stores, and is eager to sell what its databases contain. Mountains of detailed data are piling up in computers, just waiting to be mined for their commercial value," she writes.

She goes on to quote Gerald Saltzgaber, Citicorp's Point-of-Sale Information Services CEO, in saying, "Imagine how Coke would like to know the households that drink Pepsi by name and address and then be able to track them. This is target marketing based on absolute knowledge of what the household actually purchases."

> **"Customers' data will become more valuable as databases from various sites are linked. For years, banks and telecom companies have been using technology called *data mining* to track customer trends. Now, the tools are getting more powerful, and they are moving on to the Web."**
>
> *Business Week*, **April 5, 1999**
> **"Special Report: Privacy"**

Professor Mary Culnan of Georgetown University was quoted in the *Chicago Tribune* in reference to this technology at the retail level: "Little by little," she said, "the stores track who you are and what you buy. When they put all this data together, they know an awful lot about you ... The only way to keep your privacy is to drop out of the credit economy — pay cash."

Where is all this headed as we use our shoppers' card? *Popular Science* of January 1997 paints one scenario: "Never mind the 'paper or plastic' dilemma. Your supermarket checkout clerk may soon be asking you questions like this: *Mr. Kowalski, the computer says you normally buy Twinkies and Diet Coke on Fridays — did you forget them?*

"By matching the product scanning data with identities, stores can create customer profiles and more finely target their marketing directly at you. Eventually, this sort of **customer intimacy**, as some in the retail business refer to it, could lead to supermarkets printing out personalized shopping lists for you as you enter the store, or mailing you customized coupon flyers."

To a certain degree and in some areas of the country, that is already being done. In a growing number of cases, what has long been called "junk mail" arriving in the middle of the week can no longer be considered junk, or useless, simply because every coupon ad in your mailbox — you ordered!

Try this test: compare *your* junk mail packet with that of your neighbors on either side and across the street. Are your packets *exactly* alike? Chances are, they aren't! It's called *focused* marketing, *minority* marketing, even *intimacy* marketing — a number of things. The point is, "they" know your habits and shopping preferences. "They" know how to fill your pantry and how often it needs to be filled.

Snoopers Get Even More Personal

> **"Has technology brought us to the portal of a brave new world of telecommunications, or are we entering the dark place — an Orwellian society where 'Big Brother' is watching us?"**
>
> *Progressive Grocer* magazine
> "Big Brother is Watching"
> February 1997

This "we know how you live" technology becomes even more sinister through another hi-tech phenomena known as **narrowcasting**.

Here is a technique specific to the cable, satellite and digital broadcast industry with "the ability to *aim* a radio or TV program or programming at a specific, limited audience or consumer market."

It's a tool within the marketing industry also known as *narrowcast advertising* or *minority marketing*. By virtue of its individualized demographics capabilities, narrowcasting can present "virtual ads" that are specifically designed with an individual household in mind ... several hundreds or thousands of households, each with their own individualized ads, coming in over the exact same program as all the other homes on the block.

"If you've been keeping up with sports lately, you may not have noticed the increasing number of virtual advertisements," reports the November 1998 issue of *MoneyWorld* magazine. "That is because virtual ads look like a regular billboard ad to television viewers, but fans at the actual game can't see the ad. The ads seem real and appear relative to a camera's zoom effects, yet they are blocked out by any action that passes in front of them."

Experts in the field liken this technology to that of the military's smart missiles. Certain demographic data is fed into a computer that contains selective files of citizens within, say, a suburban section of a city or a special interest group. Advertisers buy a "block" of viewers like they would zip code mailing lists. Commercials are tailor-made to fit the tastes and buying habits of select individuals within the selected block, based on data collected from local grocery store computers and the activities of customers' loyalty cards.

So, during a *Monday Night Football* or World Series Baseball game, for instance, ten or more houses on any given street in any neighborhood might all be tuned into the same event. Each house could, most feasibly, see very different ads on stadium billboards and fences, or receive a different set of commercials than its neighbors in the course of any set of commercial breaks.

Read the novel *Red Mercury* by journalist Max Barclay and see how narrowcasting is used to save the city of Atlanta during the 1996 Olympic Games. It makes for a fascinating introduction to the art.

Tracking Many, Finding One

The ever-growing and evolving Information Superhighway, which includes all that is both wired and wireless communication technology, has given rise to the most outstanding Big Brother system imaginable. Cradle-to-grave dossiers on multiplied millions of individuals world-wide is now the norm. Information networks now circle the globe speeding data from home to office, from office to headquarters, from headquarters to the classroom, from the classroom to the satellite, from the satellite to millions of linked conclaves below. Private networking eventually gives way to open inter-networking which, in turn, paves the way toward regional, national and global centralization.

Congressman Bob Wise (D-WVa), quoted in *TIME* magazine in

their November 11, 1991 edition, in a cover story article entitled, "No Place To Hide": "Privacy watchdogs are warning that the combination of invasive technologies and lax laws threatens to make the U.S. a nation of people who live in glass houses, their every move open to scrutiny by outsiders."

"The law right now does not look good for privacy plaintiffs," says Andrew McClurg, law professor for the University of Arkansas and author of a study into privacy issues in 1992.

Indeed! *The Guardian* of **London** reported in a September 24, 1997 article entitled, "Cops Call the Shots," that police there were logging so many requests to the British Telephone Company (BT) for the telephone records of private citizens as to cause hundreds or even thousands of innocent citizens finding themselves caught up in a single crime investigation.

And, the snooping doesn't stop there, *The Guardian* reported. "Not just phone calls are now logged into police computers, it was revealed. All vehicles entering or leaving the City of London or British seaports are being watched by robot automatic number plate scanners (ANPS), which feed the data to the Police National Computer (PNC) in Hendon. The PNC replies within five seconds if the vehicles are *of interest* to police."

Likewise, according to the report, "details of customers' calls" are further gathered through the installation of "automated computer-to-computer *interface*" programming ... the science of word mining. The words of a conversation are subjected to an existing database of suspicious words and thoughts, then matched in such a way as to determine a specific profile of prejudice or political sway. "Unlike telephone tapping, warrants are not required before confidential data is sent out by the BT," the article's author, Duncan Campbell, writes.

But that's not all. The Brits carry all of this even further. "The data is sifted and transformed into pictorial networks and charts of who talks to whom. To these are added bank records, housing information, vehicle details, and information from inquiries, newspapers, the Net and informants. The resulting charts are often so comprehensive and complex," Campbell writes, "as to back up the most robust of paranoid nightmares."

Once such information is logged into the PNC, then the agency makes that same data available to all police agencies across the nation.

"The applications for this technology are endless," notes Dave Evans, president/CEO for Technology Recognition Systems in the *Auto I.D. News* article on faceprints. "We envision a day when consumers won't need cards at ATMs."

Bringing it All Together

And ... the *point* to it all (as we, once more, return to the main highway of *Internet Ubiquity*) is the fact that <u>*ALL*</u> of this technological advancement is linkable to the Internet! But, what does that mean? What does it mean to have all this information about us *on the Net*?

Lest we forget, the Internet is a *world* of computers networked together by way of *rooms* of computers ... larger-than-life-sized rooms that contain literally hundreds of computer systems under one roof. They're known as *data centers, digital engine rooms,* or simply, *server farms* — "digital storehouses of personal information," as reported in the May 19, 1999 edition of the *New York Times*.

In discussing these "server farms" in an article entitled, "Computing Centers Become The Keeper of Web's Future," the *Times* reported that "the Internet is fueling a re-centralization of information and a revival of big iron computing."

Pressing the point further, the *Times* went on to say that "the Internet holds the promise of anytime, anywhere access to information delivered over powerful networks to an array of information appliances like hand-held devices, cell phones with screens and television set-top boxes. They will join personal computers more than replace them anytime soon."

What's happening is a return to the *mainframe* way of doing things. Rather than housing a world of information on PCs and micro-cassettes, large capacity supersystem mainframes will become the brains of the new ubiquitous global communication network. We've dubbed these *cyborg centers* as **CenCom** systems — regional, national and international *Central Computer* centers that will store personal information and track the whereabouts of literally every individual on earth.

"The new model of computing — a proliferation of information appliances linked by the Internet to server farms — has been called the *post-PC era*," the *Times* article reported. "The evolution toward the Internet model, most analysts agree, represents the most significant change in the industry since the PC replaced the mainframe as the center of gravity in computing two decades ago."

Andrew S. Grove is quoted in the article as saying that the changes that are coming will render a whole new identity to the so-called "PC Industry."

"It probably won't even be called the PC industry," he says. "It will become the *Web Infrastructure Industry*."

Finding the Needle in the Haystack

Into this new world of Information Technology comes the Orwellian ability to find, by way of extraordinary telecommunications technology — that needle in the haystack ... *one* individual among a mass of six billion or more ... from *one* location! The summation of this chapter is laid forth in this one frightening fact — soon, and very soon, there will be no place to hide!

The reason this chapter is longer than the rest is because *that* point had to be proven with solid evidence to show what awaits us behind the *embedded Internet*. For all its benefits and promised conveniences, the *Ubiquitous Computing Era (UCE)* threatens to be all that George Orwell predicted it would be ... and then some.

We close this chapter with two compelling reports that speak directly to this point of searching for and finding *one* specific individual in a world of so many, and how super advanced and centralized technology lends a hand.

... The Most Tracked Man on Earth

He's being called *"the most tracked man in America"* — perhaps even the world. He's Wesley Wayne Miller, a sixteen year veteran of the Texas prison system. He was released to the Tarrant County Jail on Friday, May 22, 1998 and placed under the tightest tracking security system ever applied to any prisoner anywhere.

"Satellites will log his location every four seconds," reports the Associate Press story of Sunday, May 17. "If he (Miller) ever approaches forbidden locations such as the homes or workplaces of people who have asked to be protected from him, an alarm will go off."

"I believe it is safe to say it is a truly unique situation," noted David Smith, president of the Boulder, CO company providing the conventional electronic anklet. "I've never heard of an individual being placed on three different types of monitoring."

Aside from the usual ankle monitor, Wilson must also carry a pager 24 hours a day. When he calls his parole officer, "voice recognition technology will make sure it is really him calling," the *Houston Chronicle* article reported. "At all times, he will be hooked to an electronic monitor on one ankle and a satellite tracking device on the other."

The monitoring is part of the state's Super-Intensive Supervision Program, in which 1,000 Texas inmates are being monitored. ABS, Inc. of Omaha, NE, is providing the satellite tracking system in this instance. The company acknowledges that there were, as of May, "about a dozen people in New Jersey, Kansas and Iowa also under satellite surveillance."

This is the same type of technology that enabled researchers from Stanford University to undertake a bold project in 1996 that had gained them increased research dollars and the praise of colleagues around the world.

Led by their instructor, Dr. Barbara Block, the team captured and tagged 200 of the world's most expensive fish, the Bluefin Tuna. These large, 300- to 500-pound class delicacies were fitted with two kinds of computerized tags: 40 pop-up tags that would break away from the fish once information had been gathered, and 160 permanent implants that would continue to communicate with satellites until the fish was caught.

According to the Oct. 27, 1997 *New York Times*, the permanent tags "provided researchers with the first moment-by-moment chronicle of six months in a bluefin tuna's travels."

Dr. Eric Prince, co-director of the $550,000 project, commented that, "When you know what the animal is doing every two minutes, nothing can compare with that."

... Satellite Tracking Proves Deadly Accurate

On Sunday, April 22, 1996, satellite tracking proved particularly accurate in the Chechen war of resistance against the former Soviet Union. Resistance leader Dzhokhor Dudayev was in his army jeep outside his headquarters in the village of Gekhi-Chu.

According to the *L. A. Times* news article, "the fatal weapon was a missile programmed to home in on the briefcase-sized satellite phone that Dudayev was using in a field" at the time. "Two missiles fired from an aircraft were electronically guided to the phone by signals bouncing between the portable phone's antenna and a space satellite."

One man ... alone ... on the phone ... eliminated ... by satellite-guided missiles. Never before in the history of man have we had such capabilities. Where do we go from here?

- - - - - - - - - - - - - - - - - -

"Open up in there! The census taker wants to know what time you leave for work. Giant marketing firms want to know how often you use your credit cards. Your boss would like your psychological profile, your bill-paying history and a urine sample. Is that enough to make you feel like hiding in a corner, muttering to yourself about invasions of privacy? Forget it — the neighbors might be videotaping."

— **TIME** magazine
November 11, 1991
"No Place to Hide"

Chapter 7

What's It All About?
Where Do We Go From Here?
The *Final* Evolution?

We close as we opened — asking the question, *Where are we going with all this?* Is the Internet expanding? Yes!

Is the Internet evolving? In a non-natural, non-biological way, absolutely! It is <u>not</u> a living organism. It is a growing network of networks that is encompassing the world.

If it is, therefore, true that the Internet is both growing and evolving, the natural question to follow would be — *toward what?* To what end is found the destiny of the Information Superhighway? *Everything that goes up, must come down*, the old adage says. *Nothing lasts forever,* another one says. Likewise, *nothing grows without end.*

Throughout this treatise the point has been this: The Internet, as grand and marvelous a tool as it is, carries within its very nature the potential for great and grave abuse.

Advancing technology is one of the world's most commonly sought after desires. It's the aphrodisiac of dictators and despots that makes them deities in their own sight. Given the technical ability to effectively manage its affairs by knowing the intimate details of its own population and that of its subjects, it's doubtful that even Rome — or any other empire for that matter — would ever have ceased to exist. Great empires of the past fell because, in part, they deteriorated from within due to the physical limitations in their ability to effectively communicate and, hence, manipulate their own forces beyond the manageable confines of their immediate control.

In other words, they reached the limits of their technology to adequately and effectively rule and control that which they conquered and possessed.

What Guarantees Are There?

Knowing these things historically, can we hang our hopes on the *guarantee* that there will **never, ever,** be another Hitler, Stalin or Mussolini? — Ever? Will there never, ever, be another *great* dictator who will be "the man for the hour" — a product of the times?

Never? ... For sure? ... How can we be so certain?

Did the German people know that, when they elected a new Chancellor, they were birthing a dictator? To this very hour, Adolf Hitler is the blackest scar on the face of an otherwise hospitable nation.

How about the Russian people? Are the common folk of Russia's villages and towns really like the murderous dictators that have ruled over them for almost a century?

What guarantees are there that the world will **never, ever** grant both podium and power to one charismatically persuasive orator to be their leader of passion and vision, only to have him change colors before their worshipful eyes and seek to devour them all?

According to National Defense Council Foundation, the year 1997 witnessed no less than 68 world conflicts lasting a year or more. Since 1989 (the end of the Cold War), over 4 million people have lost their lives to war and warlike skirmishes.

Associated Press—January 1, 1998

What *guarantees* are there that this will never happen again ... and that it will not happen this next time on a global scale ... *one man* ruling all nations ...?

The U.N. you say? The United Nations — and other peacekeeping organizations that are in place like unto it — will see to it that another Hitler never comes forth, you say.

Is that true?

You *are* aware, aren't you, that the U.N. was established on the premise that its very existence would rid the world of war. And, given that *fact*, you are also painfully aware of the fact that there have been more wars fought and more lives lost *since* the creation of the U.N. than there ever were *before* it was created — aren't you?

What's the Point?

So, why are we belaboring this point? What correlation is there between a world at war and the embedded Internet? Simply this: by design, the Internet at-large, and its ubiquitous second life, is destined for some form of *global centralization.*

It's not our goal to convince people *not* to use the Internet — that's an impossible fantasy at this late stage. No, our simple goal in all this has been to produce a wiser, smarter, more knowledgeable user who is not blind to *all* the potentials of a tool as encompassing as the 'Net. Do not be lured by its charm ... there's a larger agenda to it all than meets the eye. Be restrictive in your pursuits of all it has to offer and all that it promises to provide.

The Grander Agenda

By virtue of the Internet's very existence and its utility in the world of business, the entire global corporate landscape is changing virtually overnight. All the "old" rules are being rewritten and repackaged relevant to a more real global mentality than has ever existed before.

In business seminars, government workshops and academic conferences all across this land today there is an underlying message going forth that is directing everybody's attention away from *national sovereignty* and onto *global governance.* In like manner, the treatises and white paper reports produced *for* and *through* these conferences are experiencing a second life through re-publication in the nation's major publications and as books on best seller lists.

The logic behind these new courses of study is pure and simple: that which is birthed of the simple evolves toward the complex. And, along the way, there is ever-increasing turmoil, stress, pressure, change. As the lesser "evolves" into the greater, the older yields reluctantly to the younger. There is philosophical, psychological, emotional, physical conflict in the transformation. Prior to the surrender usually comes disagreement, conflict, war and death.

Once the winds of change begin to blow, the "old" world view usually loses ground to the "new" world view, and a new world order rises from the sea and becomes the ruling beast of a new status quo. Politically, scientifically and sociologically, the process is known as *Entropy* — or, the Second Law of Thermodynamics.

This law simply states that as one moves from order, increasing disorder is experienced. In a global sense, as civilized man becomes more advanced in his government, his life-style, his science and his sophistication, the more turmoil in his environment and his society he will experience ... until such a day as new order justifiably replaces the old order, then the process begins anew.

It's an old proverb: you don't put new wine in old bags without the old bags bursting asunder, spilling the new upon the ground. You either reinforce the old bags before introducing the new wine, or you throw the old bags away and replace them with new.

Today, before our very eyes, that old adage is being played out as a new world order — complete with its younger politicians, new policies, new technology and new ways — encroaches upon old empires and regimes.

It's like watching the introduction of a color dye into a pail of water. The new dye advances like an unhindered cloud through the water, until all of the old becomes the color of the new.

For the sake of our topic here, the *evolving* Internet is itself a symbol of the world's *evolution* into a new tomorrow ... a new world order, if you will, that now is right around the next corner. The Embedded, Ubiquitous Internet is more than mere technological advancement. It's a statement ... a proclamation ... an announcement that cries for all to hear. It's echoing the words of those we quoted in Chapter One —

Alvin Toffler (FUTURE SHOCK): "We are creating a *new* society. Not a changed society. Not an extended, larger-than-life version of our present society. But a _new_ society!"

... again: "A _new civilization_ is emerging in our lives ... This new civilization brings with it *new* family styles, *changed ways* of working, loving and living; a *new* economy, *new* political conflicts, and, beyond all this, an *altered* consciousness as well."

Richard Louv : "The America we know is dying, but a second America is rising from the body of the first ... America II."

This *new* Internet is being driven, it seems, by a wild, maddening *spirit* running throughout the land — around the world — that makes life itself too difficult, too stressed out, too unbearable. There is a cry for order coming from everywhere, but it's nowhere to be found.

"Each day we awake to a world that appears more confused and disordered than the one we left the night before. Nothing seems to work anymore. Our lives are bound up in constant repair. We are forever mending and patching. Our leaders are forever lamenting and apologizing. Every time we think we've found a way out of a crisis, something backfires. The powers that be continue to address the problems at hand with solutions that create even greater problems than the ones they were meant to solve.

"Everywhere we go, we find ourselves waiting in lines or pushed into corners. Things about us continue to accelerate, yet nothing seems to be getting done anywhere. We are bogged down, the society is bogged down; and all of a sudden we get this urge to trample over everything in our path, leaving the world behind us in disarray."

That was **_Jeremy Rifkin_** in his best-seller, ENTROPY: A NEW WORLD VIEW. He hit it right on the head, didn't he? You wonder what's going on with the new social phenomena known as "road rage" and "going postal"? There it is! The whole world is coming to the end of itself, and it's running scared. It's rapidly running out of answers and it doesn't know who to turn to for both reasons and solutions.

So, to whom are they turning? Well, the business seminars are still playing to packed houses. The fastest selling non-fiction books today are self-help, psychology and (believe it or not) religion (especially *prophecy*). Psychic hotlines and infomercials on television are raking in billions of dollars a year. There is no clear-cut winner or front runner that we can see that is seizing the market on providing the right answers to a world of enquiring, helpless, frightened minds.

In the midst of it all, however, is the beast of Technology. It is here, in advancing technology, that modern man is finding (at best) superficial peace, tranquility and personal control. Technology is the *perfect* slave. It does nothing until a button is pushed. Then, it's at your every beck and call. Whatever it is you need or desire, the right technology will deliver it to you in pristine condition. No questions. No quarrels. No objections. Just perfect obedience. No guilt. No hassles.

But — the *world* itself is in need of *global* solutions with *universal* applications. The problems can't be solved off the retail shelves of hi-tech stores. That's not to say that the *tools* by which and through which the solutions are applied aren't found there ... they are. But the real solutions to a world breaking apart at the seams are found elsewhere and they must be centrally administered. And, that's where the next step in the Internet evolution becomes revolutionary! *Global centralization!* You have here a network given to being centralized at its best! What do you do with it?

Logic of the Future!

Once again, this *Going Global* concept is being taught everywhere these days, at virtually every strata of society — from both the top down and the bottom up. Not only at the corporate level and at the self-help sales seminars, but in our public schools and universities throughout the land. See if you can follow the logic of the future ... see if you can follow the pattern of new solutions to old and current problems from the perspective of "global governance":

The Logic Supporting Globally Centralized Governance

Borderless Networking — Through the auspices of a ubiquitous global communication system comes the reality of global networking.

Standardization — Through borderless networking comes the *need* for common standards for all.

Administration — Through common standards comes the *need* to oversee adherence to those standards; hence, centralized administration.

Consolidation — Through centralized administration of global common standards comes the call for consolidation.

Governance — Control is applied; rule is established; a government is born.

Supporters of Global Logic

"There's no shirking the conclusion that international peace cannot be permanent without a *world state*," wrote Hans J. Morgenthau in his book, POLITICS AMONG NATIONS. "There is also no shirking the further conclusion that in no period of human history was civilization more in need of permanent peace and, hence, *a world state*."

"The only possible way to make global decisions to global

problems is to take a global approach," states an editorial by the late chairman of Fiat and Olivetti corporations, Aurelio Peccei, who was also head of The Club of Rome at the time, in the *Toronto Globe & Mail* newspaper. "A new international order will have to be established, not just in the economic sphere, but in the social and political areas as well."

"When the whole world begins to break down and fall apart, then we must look to the way the whole world has been organized, because that's where the problem lies," writes Rifkin in ENTROPY. "At present, no single leader or ideology on this planet can effectively address the universal crisis at-hand, because all are committed to the existing world view, one that is diseased and dying and is contaminating everything it gave birth to," he writes.

One World? Seriously?

It's literally *everywhere* we turn these days. "Global" this and "global" that. Interdependence. Global Village. Global Networking. International Community. Global Governance ...

Are they really serious about all this? What are they telling us ... that, after all these years of denying the very possibility and likelihood of it all, the world is *actually* moving (or, being driven) into some sort of *one world system*? Is it truly happening? If so, what does it all mean? What are the benefits and the consequences? What's it all about?

Peter Drucker, in MANAGING IN TURBULENT TIMES, writes: "Economically, the world has become integrated and inter-dependent as never before. There is now a true *world economy*, which is moving toward a *transnational money* that is increasingly independent of — or, at least, uncoupled from — any national currency. There is no more *key currency*. The traditional concept of economic sovereignty is fast becoming a mockery."

Nation-States Give Way to Global Villages

The world of economics and high technology is changing the face of the world at-large ... so much so, that contemporary arguments now ask the viable question, "Why wait any longer? Let's make the switch now! What are we waiting for?"

Today's sociological architects are pleading for a whole new world! A world of *friction free* (digital) economics, *direct democracy* via all-electronic polling and a *telematic* society in which everyone everywhere lives in a high surveillance electronic glass bowl.

"*Commerce* is everywhere identical," notes a British brochure titled, "The Assimilation of the English and American Money as a Step Toward a Universal Money."

"Buying and selling, lending and borrowing, are alike all the world over, and all matters concerning them ought universally to be alike too. Ultimately," the pamphlet goes on to say, "the world will see *one Code of Commerce, and one money as the symbol of it.*"

Quoting Mark Stahlman, president of New Media Associates (New York), in *Information Week* on February 17, 1997: "everyone who speaks authoritatively about politics and computers seems to agree that technology will increase the capability for *direct* (as opposed to *representative*) *democracy* and will diminish the relevance of 'nations' in an increasingly global economy. In the now-standard Information Age view, *America* is obsolete, as are all nation-states."

Amazing! He goes on to say, "*Nations* are viewed as passe', second wave, and a hindrance at best. The technocrats — from whatever party or organization — are opposed to forming '*a more perfect Union.*'"

"The technology of printing came into being in the same era as the *nation-state*," Anthony Smith says in THE GEOPOLITICS OF INFORMATION, "and both seem to be reaching the end of their usefulness in the era of the computer; it is physically impossible to impose upon data the same kinds of controls that are imposed upon goods and paper-borne information."

Smith goes on to make the argument that, in this hi-speed, hi-tech world, "there is no room in the long run for *conflicting information doctrines* within a world which is becoming increasingly interconnected."

In other words, the differences that divide the world into its various nation-state boundaries are no longer acceptable, Smith and others are writing. Such divisions are time-consuming and trivial when compared to the greater issues having to do with global interconnectivity, e-commerce, interactive and embedded silicon chips, and much more. Here we have a world that, for all sakes of practicality, should be coming together under one economy, one anthem and one "global-centric" domestic policy, yet we're still fighting over land rights and socio-religious prejudices, they say.

"The world is in the process of becoming a *global village*," asserts Stewart Brand in THE MEDIA LAB: INVENTING THE FUTURE AT MIT.

"The world's cities are more alike every year," he writes. "They are so intensely linked with each other that they increasingly act, and look, like boroughs of one large city which is situated everywhere and nowhere."

Let's camp here for a moment longer. He has some intriguing observations about a global embedded communications network.

"One creation of the *supercity* is the multinational corporation," he goes on to say. "While nations fade, the world corporations are increasing robustly, many of them now larger in financial terms than many nations. The world supercity is not the capital of anything, except itself.

"Global transactions are not conducted at a leisurely rural or even suburban pace, but on the schedule depicted by the Texan phrase for haste: *in a hot New York minute*. The pace of cities and the pace of computers were made for each other. *What I want, I want now!* Computers deliver in nanoseconds."

"Rather than functioning as discrete nation-states, each isolated and buffered from the ups and downs of its neighbors, countries have now become increasingly *irrelevant*, economically speaking," writes Joel Kurtzman, executive editor for *Harvard Business Review*, in his book, THE DEATH OF MONEY. "Borders have been breached. Signals bounced off satellites or hurled through undersea cables do not wait at a customs house to clear. In fact, it is now far easier and faster to move $1 billion from New York to Tokyo than to move a truckload of lettuce or grapes across the California - Arizona line.

"In reality, markets everywhere are now linked. We are all on the *megabyte standard.*

"The *(new) world economy* is likely to unfold when bankers, investors, traders, policy analysts, government officials, economists, financial experts, and corporate leaders are all linked together like dendrites in the brain."

"The Internet is in the process of becoming a mass market. The public is flocking online by the millions. It's that growing audience which makes the Internet tick. "

The Industry Standard
June 28, 1999

GLOBALIZATION! Can it be true? To be perfectly honest, it's hard ... no, it's almost impossible ... to imagine. What does this long word — this *globalization* concept — really mean? The "end" of nation-states. A *global village*?!

"Orwellian Mischief" Looming Ahead?

In a 1994 court case dealing with the question of police arrests that are made based on erroneous computer information, Supreme Court Justice Ruth Ginsburg commented that "as automation increasingly invades modern life, the potential for *Orwellian mischief* grows!" Indeed, as technology itself becomes more advanced, society as a whole is increasingly compressed into neat little boxes of conformity.

And, as *conformity* expands and spreads like a silent virus, its gluttony is at the expense of *liberty.* And, as more and more liberty increasingly becomes less and less, *conformity* begins to look and sound a lot more like *slavery.* Once slavery becomes entrenched within the society, *demagoguery* rules.

> **"In a society where knowledge is power, centralized knowledge is centralized power. "**
>
> —*Richard Sobel*
> Berkman Center for Internet & Society
> Harvard Law School
> *N. Y. Times* - May 19, 1999

The "Tools of Demagoguery" include *mastery of control* over the masses. The greater the tool of control, the tighter the rule of the demagogue. And, there is no greater tool of control than the *intimate knowledge* of people's private lives and the ability to use such knowledge masterfully in manipulating the private destinies of individuals ... one life at a time.

The point-of-origin behind such control rests within the fertile soils and innocent solutions of *idealism.* Once matured, the concepts of control evolve into an *agenda* which, in turn, becomes official *policy*... and, in time, the idealistic agenda-turned-policy settles itself into a *governing administration*, anchored by a *centralized bureaucracy* in possession of the finest and latest in super surveillance, telecommunication and database storage and retrieval technology anywhere (i.e.: an *embedded* Internet, for instance).

ONE Orwellian Leader on Horizon?

AURELIO PECCEI was quite a visionary and world mover. As an Italian industrialist (chairman of both Fiat and Olivetti corporations), Peccei successfully drew together the sharpest minds and most influential personalities of western Europe to deal with major issues facing all mankind. Through his efforts, the Club of Rome was started in 1968.

Peccei had no qualms about the course of mankind headed straight into the arms of disaster if something wasn't done to change the course of the nations away from the precipice of global destruction. In Peccei's view, the world-at-large needed a centralized leadership nucleus in which all nations worked together as a community, sharing common goals, common resources, and common laws.

Since 1968, the Club of Rome has been the premiere global association of nations leading in the global debate for "new world" solutions. The Club of Rome, under Peccei's leadership as its founder and president, has led the search for *a global leader* suited to administrate a *one world government.*

He always felt that, given just the right circumstances, events and personalities coming together, the world could be *made* into a far better, safer and saner place to live.

"The yeast of change does exist — albeit scattered — in the myriad spontaneous groupings of people springing up here and there, like antibodies in a sick organism," Peccei noted in a speech before the First Global Conference on the Future in Toronto, July 1980. "They are the peace movements; population policy societies; ecologists; women's lib; defenders of minorities, of human rights and of civil liberties; social workers; amnesty apostles; non-violent reformers; conscientious objectors; world federalists; and consumer advocates — just to name a few."

"The world is changing rapidly. The globalization of the economy, the fact that <u>live from now on in and *information society*</u>, the complexity and the uncertainty which are the common trademarks of the present world, lead us to take into consideration a number of these new factors. We have to understand this new data in order to have a better understanding of other cultures, other languages, other modes of reasoning. "

The Club of Rome opening statement on Webpage
<u>**http:\\www.clubofrome.org\globis_nsoc.html**</u>
"The New Global Society" page

In another global conference setting, Peccei made this observation: "I think that something is developing within modern man in such a way that ONE episode, ONE disaster, ONE *charismatic leader* — something may come one day and wake up this dormant capacity."

This "dormant capacity" he referred to was, at the time, being shaken to its very roots. The Cold War was running at fever pitch. The world saw man reach for the stars with Sputnik ... and the dividing of a nation with the Berlin Wall.

Poverty and famine was spreading like a virus upon the ground. Meanwhile, technology was growing ... and world peace was skating on thin ice at the birthing of Camelot, the New Frontier and the Peace Corps.

In the midst of all this energy, NATO wasn't quite 10 years old when Paul-Henry Spaak of Belgium came in as the second Secretary General of that post-war organization. Having previously served in the Brussels Parliament in the late-'30s, then as Belgian Prime Minister in the late-'40s, Spaak was well-seasoned in international politics and the world's search for solutions of messianic proportions.

It was while serving with NATO that Spaak made this observation of the world's need for a single leader:

"We do not want another committee. We have too many already. What we want is a man, of sufficient stature, to lift us out of this economic morass into which we are sinking. Send us such a man, and <u>whether he be god or devil</u>, we shall receive him."

TIME magazine, in its July 1, 1974 edition, featured a guest editorial that reviewed some of the world-moving accomplishments by then Secretary of State Henry Kissinger through his service to Presidents Nixon and Ford. At the conclusion of the editorial came this recommendation:

"Kissinger's achievements have, at last, justified the establishment of a new political office, which I sincerely

hope the United Nations will consider: President of the Planet Earth."

What the Star Gazers (and Other Watchers) Have Seen

In the late-1960s to mid-'70s, this reporter worked at his first post-high school big city newspaper, *The Houston Tribune* ... the city's politically conservative weekly. We, the staff and subscribers, proudly established a sub-motto to the paper: *"Houston's Second Largest Newspaper (since the other two claim to be #1)!"* The "other" two, of course, were the Post and Chronicle.

Our "#2" newspaper had a lot of history and notoriety with it. Paul Harvey had a regular column. So did Billy Graham. Several state and federal legislators wrote articles and letters to the Tribune. One of that paper's earliest editors was William C. Wood, Jr., my dad's oldest brother and former chief investigator for Jim Garrison, the New Orleans' District Attorney who challenged the Warren Report in its investigation into the Kennedy assassination. (Uncle Bill's role was depicted in the Oliver Stone film *J.F.K.* as that of Bill Boudreau.)

Aside from my uncle as editor, we had a few other "characters" around there of one sort of fame or another, one of whom was Mr. "C. E. Forsythe" — or "Frank," as I knew him. I seemed to recall he was a production manager of sorts.

"Frank" came to me one day at the office and presented an article he said he wrote under his "pen name" — C. E. Forsythe. The article appeared in the July, 1970 edition of *Horoscope* magazine, and I think it was entitled, "This Century's Most Significant Birthday (-date)."

As I read the article, I learned that astrologers around the globe were concerned about certain "signs" they had seen in the heavens on Sunday, February 4, 1962 surrounding the birth of one who, according to Forsythe, "might become the next great leader of our age."

Forsythe and others were so impressed, in fact, that the article opened with this "Public Notice," of sorts: "Do you have a child in your family or know of one in your community whose date of birth fell on or around February 4, 1962? In the United States, he would have been born at 6:17 pm, Central Standard Time."

In June, 1989, the editors of *Prophecy in the News* magazine (P.O. Box 7000; Oklahoma City, OK 73153; $12/yr) picked up this old article from HOROSCOPE and reviewed it for their audience. Quoting G. G. Stearman in his review: "One born on this day, they say, would have *idealistic, progressive and humanitarian goals*. He would be *original and inventive*, with *great mental agility and astuteness*. He would *love the unusual and the progressive*. He might be *unpredictable and unconventional*. His mind would be *prodigious* and his personality, *charismatic*.

"But he would have a dark side, too," Stearman continues. "His life might be marked by *deceit, hidden influences, the unforeseen, secretiveness, intrigue,* and even *treachery*. Such negative events might originate with the individual himself, or they might come from those who surround him."

Returning to my old friend "Frank" at the Tribune, who claimed at the time to be the same "C. E. Forsythe" who wrote this article for HOROSCOPE magazine, I asked him what he thought about all this. His response was, "I honestly don't know what to make of all this myself. I'm both baffled and a bit scared by it. I will tell you this, though. Ever since my discovery and the same by other astrologers on the subject, my wife — who has been a good Baptist girl for years — hasn't stopped talking to me about *the antichrist!* She's convinced that this is one-and-the-same."

"And you, Frank? What do you think?" I asked.

"Again, like I said, I'm not certain. But, it sure sounds awfully close to me," he said.

"Has your wife read to you about the antichrist in the Bible?" I asked.

"Yes, several times. And, just to be on the safe side, I've started going to church with her since making this discovery. I'm not saying that I've become a believer and all that, but there might be something to it all and I want to find out what it is," he said.

That was back in 1970 when all this happened. Some 20 years after this event, something else happened that reminded me of that day at the Tribune. This time, it had to do with the desertion by some military intelligence officers of their military outpost in Germany.

Newspapers across the land carried the story under sensational headlines. There were six of them — five men and one woman. At the time of their desertion, they were, according to AP news stories at the time, stationed with the 701st Military Intelligence Brigade at Augsburg, West Germany. They abandoned their posts in July, 1990.

Their capture took place a short while later near Gulf Breeze, Florida. When interrogated as to the reason for their desertion, their answer was of such a nature that both the Pentagon and the national media wanted to bury the story as quietly as possible, which is probably why the news of their capture did not make it to the front pages of the same papers that days before screamed of their desertion.

The reason for their behavior? According to the AP, "they had learned the identity of the antichrist" and were going forth to kill him! Consequently, the six were pegged as "religious fundamentalists" belonging to an "end-of-the-world cult."

As I had opportunity to both read and review this particular story, I couldn't help but be impressed with the fact that these were not your daily, run-of-the-mill normal soldiers at some out-of-the-way guard post in some distant land. These were six very highly trained, highly trusted and credentialed specialists in their field and branch of the U.S. military.

Additionally, that same AP story reported that the six had predicted some major power shifting in "Lebanon" and "the area of the Middle East" by August 4, 1990 ... and, indeed, the world witnessed the Iraqi invasion of Kuwait on August 1 and the resultant military buildup in the region following. It's cause to pause and wonder what else did these six intelligence officers know from inside Germany that would compel them to abandon their posts, virtually destroying their personal careers and private integrity.

Why did they come to the U.S. in their reported pursuit of the antichrist? How very interesting it is that this action took place when the one mysteriously born on February 4/5, 1962 would have turned 28 years of age!

Gathering Compelling Evidence

A good, professional researcher follows his leads once he has satisfied himself with the credibility of those leads. Before reporting his findings, he compiles the notes provided by those leads. The notes begin to bring order to a concept ... and the concept evolves into the story.

Throughout this treatise we have witnessed an evolution take place toward an historic conclusion. It has been established already, for instance, that the hi-tech world of supercomputers and spy satellites has a preoccupation with the concept of *global networking*. Likewise, as one follows the leads down the various corridors of thought, discussion and philosophy (for there is more philosophy and spiritism found at the core of science than one normally imagines), it's not long before the discussions on global networking turn to *globalism, supra-statism, global governance* and, eventually to *global leadership values*.

What has been most remarkable in this issue of the embedded Internet is its inescapable linkage to the politicized New World Order. What the Internet is becoming, in conclusion, is the ultimate ubiquitous network for Big Brother!

Sorry about that. Try as we did to keep the review of the subject as surface as is normally done and away from "politics," we found it extremely difficult to avoid some of the "issues" underlying the project. Despite our efforts, we found a fad with a future ... a technology linked to a transition ... and that meant *design and direction* toward a *goal!*

To talk about Big Brother is to envision the historical prophecies of *the antichrist!* And, the compelling question posed is, *"Will Antichrist be for real?"*

The Future is Clearly Understood

Of course, any discussion at this point on this matter necessitates inclusion of the Bible ... for the Bible is the one source that speaks more exclusively on these matters than any other book. In the prophecies of Daniel (Old Testament) and those of Jesus Christ, Paul the apostle and The Book of The Revelation (New Testament), there are numerous predictions of this one who would eventually come into the world to both rule and control the world from a centralized global government. This ruler who was to come is identified in the Biblical prophecies as *the antichrist*. Every novel selling on bookstore shelves, every movie produced in Hollywood, that have ever addressed this possibility (be it from a position of either fact or fiction) have always turned to the Biblical prophecies for their background material.

That raises another question: *Is the Bible wrong?* Just because it is *the Bible*, does that fact alone rule it out as being a viable resource and reference book? If so, *why?* What scientific proof is there that *proves* the Bible as being inaccurate in anything?

Take any recognized field of science — mathematics, physics, biology, earth sciences, astronomy, archeology, etc. — and see if any of these fields *can* ever or *has* ever proved the Bible inadequate, insufficient or inaccurate in any way.

Now, in all fairness, should you choose to pursue such a challenge, be absolutely certain that the authority you use to bring forth such proof is totally *without* equal representation and accreditation on the opposing side of "the evidence."

For instance, on the issue of "evolution-vs-creation," for nearly every credentialed, authorized expert there might be on the evolution side of the argument, there now seems to be a significant army of like-educated and credentialed experts on the opposing side. The men and women on the creation side of the debate are no less professional and educated for the position they hold than their evolution-believing counterparts.

So, in order to "prove" the Bible insufficient in such

matters, the practice of offering mere opinions must be abandoned and the true laws of science, reason and evidence must be applied in all fairness and balance.

The point is this: As the Bible continues to show itself viable in the fields of science, literature, the arts, and the other disciplines around us, it has likewise shown itself stalwart and trustworthy in the areas of history and, in particular, *prophecy* (history proclaimed before the fact).

Prophecy is a most peculiar practice when you study it up close and scientifically. If it's anything at all, one thing it is *not* — it is *not* opinion. Plain and simple. *True* "prophecy" — the *real* stuff that ALWAYS comes to pass — must, by its very nature, be of divine source. By its very practice and application, *prophecy* commands accountability! The reason for this is: *Prophecy* DEMANDS an answer! It can not be ignored ... nor forgotten. It's too bold to be lightly esteemed.

Real prophecy — Divine prophecy! — is in your face and will not be removed. Why? Because prophecy is a Divine proclamation of what *will* be! "It SHALL be so!" There is no speculation, no hesitation, no probabilities or possibilities about it.

Once again, *true ... real ... legitimate ... genuine* "prophecy" is Divine in its source — exclusively! — making it "a sure bet" in its assurance. Prophecy never fails ... period!

Having made that proclamation as best we can under the limitations of the printed page without resorting to sensational typefaces, we will quickly close this report with this challenge:

It's been said that approximately two-thirds of the Bible is divinely-sourced prophecy ... and roughly another two-thirds of that is designated "end-time" in specifics, meaning that the bulk of Bible prophecy is oriented to that historical time frame "immediately preceding" the prophesied Return of Christ.

Into that time frame is found the reign of *the antichrist*. In fact, the prophetic evidence points to the idea that antichrist is *pre*-Christ, meaning that when the antichrist comes onto the scene, the very next major world event will be the Second Coming of Christ!

If these things be true, and if what the world of Bible prophecy is talking about as they unashamedly discuss the so-called "signs of the times" as truly being the "times of the end," then the question remaining for every man, woman and child on the planet is, *"What are we to do with this evidence?"*

Indeed, what are we to do in the face of the possible fulfillment of that which remains to be fulfilled? Are we simply living in a world of happenstance? Are things just going along life's merry way, having no real design or purpose or direction? Is life really so empty? Are the social psychotherapists and behavioral scientists correct when they tell us *"there are no absolutes ... there is no ultimate, cosmic accountability to which we must answer!"*?

We belabor this point for this reason: If Bible prophecy has *always* been proven true and accurate in all cases, then what makes us think it *won't* be true in its assessment of time and history coming to an end?

And, if the Bible has *always* been true in these things, is it possible that it might be true in all other things as well — such as how we are to live our lives in preparation for Christ's return and a glorious eternal future — ?

I realize these are religious matters ... but, they are legitimate issues if, indeed, the affairs of men and their history are in the hands of history's God.

If God is real, and if He is relevant to the current times, then *all* matters of earthly life are of spiritual concern, for it is the mundane matters of this life that influence what we do, the way we are, and what we become. Taken on such a personal level ... such affairs become spiritual matters to us.

Approaching life's final decisions from a different perspective for a moment — what do I risk if, at the end of it all, I come to the end of my life and I suddenly *do* find myself standing before a *real* God — the one and only *true* God — just as the Bible said I would eventually do.

What if this true God *does* ask me certain questions

pertinent to the doctrines of scripture, especially those concerning Christ, Whom He called His "only begotten Son"?

What happens if, despite all my reasoning while I was alive on this earth, I suddenly find that *everything* the Bible ever said within its covers proved to be *absolutely* true?

What do I risk not believing any of it?

What do I stand to lose if I'm proven wrong and God is proven right?

"For the scientist who has lived by his faith in the power of reason, the story ends like a bad dream. He has scaled the mountains of ignorance; he is about to conquer the highest peak. As he pulls himself over the final rock, he greeted by a band of theologians who have been sitting there for centuries."

—Robert Jastrow
astronomer
Reader's Digest 1980
"Have Astronomers Found God?"

"Yes, the Net has changed the rules. For good. If we're to thrive, or even survive, we must live, eat, and breathe the Net. Starting yesterday."

—Robert D. Hof
Business Week
"E-Biz" section, p.EB 9
March 22, 1999

"And he causeth all, both small and great, rich and poor, free and bond, to receive a mark in their right hands, or in their foreheads; And that no man might buy or sell, save he that had the mark, or the name of the beast, or the number of his name.

—Revelation 13:16-17
The Bible (KJV)

NYS·TEC *Update - Fall 1997*

SMART TOILETS AND DUMB TERMINALS:
THE FUTURE OF TECHNOLOGY

In early June, a couple of us from NYSTEC journeyed to Atlanta for Comdex/Spring '97, one of the computer industry's largest annual conventions. We set out for Dixie hoping to sneak a peek at the future of technology.

We found plenty of prognosticators at Comdex who were eager to share their views about the future of computing and technology in general. Prophets ranged from voluble high-tech hucksters on the exhibition floor to glib industry magnates in prearranged confabs with titles such as "The Hottest Technology Trends," "Where Next The Web" and "Future Directions in Games."

We've decided to share some of the most agreed-upon predictions heard at Comdex/Spring '97. Collectively these predictions paint a kind of impressionistic picture of technological life in the early 21st Century.

> *Tiny computers will monitor everything from road conditions to machine vibrations to the growth and infestation of crops.*

A session entitled "The Crystal Ball - Headlines from 2002" provided the most entertaining predictions in Atlanta. This session involved six technology experts who pretended to travel back in time from the year 2002 to describe the significant high-tech events that they supposedly witnessed over the next five years. Participants were Tom Koulopoulos of Delphi Consulting Group , Tim Bajarin of Creative Strategies Research, Christine Comaford of planetU, Dr. Norman Gaut of Picture Tel Corp., author Geoffrey James, and David Moschella of Computerworld magazine.

Perhaps the wildest prediction involved toilets, which in a few short years will evidently do a whole lot more than just flush. Assuming you choose to buy one, your toilet of the future will be equipped with digital sensors that will detect and analyze health problems by breaking down the chemical composition of human waste. If necessary, your Big Brother toilet will even send an emergency message to your doctor via the Internet.

If having your toilet linked to the Internet doesn't thrill you, then how about your refrigerator? In a few years you'll be able to call up your fridge from the office, ask it to examine its contents, and based on the available items, it will recommend recipes for dinner. It will even contact the grocery store and have items waiting for you when you go shopping.

Sensor-based devices such as refrigerators, toilets, cameras and other machines will constitute most of the stuff linked to the computer networks of the future. In fact, many pundits predict that a surge of non-human traffic on the Internet will be prompted by the expiration of Moore's Law early next decade. Moore's Law states that every 18 months or so, a new and improved memory chip comes along with twice the capacity of its predecessor. Up until just recently, many experts believed that the memory chip would soon reach its physical limits. However, the latest advances suggest that chip capacity will soon increase at a much faster rate than is posited by Moore's Law.

Whether or not Moore's Law actually expires, chip prices should decline precipitously. Lower prices will enable us to embed these chips and sensors in roads, walls, fields, cars, planes just about everywhere. This will create a new worldwide network of tiny computers that will monitor everything from road conditions to machine vibrations to the growth and infestation of crops. Information collected by these computerized minimachines will be transmitted over a new global network similar to — and probably linked to — the Internet.

Appendix 1 - "Smart Toilets"

Eventually a majority of homes and offices will be connected to the Internet via fiberoptic lines, but this won't occur until 2010 at the earliest. In the meantime, one or more products will emerge from the alphabet soup of competitive telecommunications (PCS, ISDN, ADSL, etc.) to provide a much faster connection from your home or business to the Information Superhighway. Whether these new, wider pipelines are wireless or copper-wire based, they should stifle everybody's main complaint about the Internet: that it's way too slow. Increased bandwidth will also allow for the installation of high - resolution video phones in homes and offices. Video conferencing will become so popular it could even pose a threat to commercial air travel.

> ***The smartcard will enable you to do your personal computing from any location. Never again will you need to haul around a heavy laptop.***

The network computer (NC) is another innovation many experts believe will gain widespread popularity early next century. Most experts expect the NC to gradually supplant the PC. Software will reside on networks and not on PC hard drives. Software revisions will happen without you noticing. Software product life-cycles will be counted in weeks, not months, and software will be dirt-cheap. Sometime between 2005 and 2010, dumb network terminals will overtake 80% of the market.

Perhaps the most revolutionary innovation over the next five years will be the introduction of the smartcard. By 2002, everybody will carry a small smartcard with a personal profile saved in its memory. Whether you're in a hotel, a public building, an airport, or at someone else's home or business, you'll be able to plug your smartcard into any standard computer terminal and it will display your personalized desktop. These dumb terminals will be as ubiquitous as TV sets are today. However, security on the Net will be a major problem. People will pay big bucks for privacy.

Appendix 1 - "Smart Toilets"

Mark Twain once said that a genuine expert can foretell a thing that's 500 years away far easier than a thing that's only 500 seconds off. After comparing past technology prognostications to actual events, it's a good bet that our most important future advancements weren't even mentioned at Comdex/Spring '97. Whether or not these Comdex predictions actually come true, they were irresistibly fun to hear.

http://www.nystec.com/nwsfal97/fal97_02.html

New York Technology Enterprise Corp.
75 Electronic Parkway
Rome NY 13441
(315)338-5818

Reviewing World News of a World in Transition

Trans-World

MONITOR

Transition Research * P. O. Box 42005 * Houston, TX 77242
713/782-1304 * 713/953-0512 fax
<u>Web</u>: _http://www.transrez.com_ * <u>E-mail</u>: transrez@transrez.com

<u>August 1999</u>

New Molecular Computers Announced!

Can you imagine owning a computer that does all that a computer can do — and not see it? It could become the hit of every party. Of course, we can't begin to imagine how such computers could be of practical use, given the fact that whatever computer we wish to sit down to, we do just that. We sit down at a keyboard, flip a switch and watch a monitor. Hence, the relationship begins and is maintained. We hit a few keys, click an attached (or wireless) mouse, and watch a monitor. So, the idea of possessing and using a computer that is barely visible (and, in some applications, is not visible) is beyond us.

And, yet, that is exactly what is being introduced to the world right now. It's a new phenomena known, among other things, as organic circuitry, in which researchers at Hewlett-Packard announce that there will eventually be "many Pentiums on a grain of sand"

In the July 15, 1999 issue of Science, researchers at Hewlett-Packard and UCLA announced the development as one that would eventually lead to "ultra-tiny processors 100 billion times faster than the most

UCLA researcher Pat Collier holds a chip containing the first single layer molecular circuitry.
- DARPA photo

powerful ones available today," reported ABC News.

"We could have a prototype of a molecular computer in five years and something you might imagine buying in 10," notes HP researcher and article author, Philip Kuekes.

MNBC News online reports that researchers said they found "a way to construct the circuits using a chemical process, making the switches as small as a molecule. They believe the process could lead to components much smaller than today's smallest transistors."

"These things are small," Kuekes says. "We're literally talking about computers woven into your clothing or painted on a wall."

Virtually Limitless Applications

Researchers suggest that such molecular computer chips could have unbelievable applications in the field of medicine. Such a microscopic sensor could come along side a particular breed of bacteria and, quite possibly, identify the bacteria or disease. In fact, patterned after today's new breed of unique time-release or "need-release" application patches, such molecular computer chips could feasibly be used to administer medications ... internally!

Although researchers have not yet tried such applications, Kuekes suggests it is not outside the realm of possibility. "It's got interesting biomedical implications," he says. "We haven't done it, but it's truly a plausible technology."

The capabilities of this technology could even see hard disks "that never fill up," they say. Eventually, says UCLA chemistry professor

James Heath, such molecular technology — known in some circles as nanotechnology — could "replicate the power of 100 computer workstations in a space the size of a grain of salt."

These new chips "could be as small as a grain of dust," Kuekes adds. "When you walk into a room, it will turn the TV to your favorite channel. Or, instead of getting carpal tunnel syndrome pushing a mouse around, your finger becomes the mouse. "

Smaller Technology Places the Net on Your Body

"Now you can target potential customers no matter where they are — whether they're in the car, out shopping, or in the kitchen," announced the August 1999 edition of *New Media* magazine. "Access to the Internet will be as easy as reaching into your pocket. We have the ability to make a computing world that is smaller, faster ... better. The new bionic world of info appliances will potentially allow users to access any information from any place at any time with any device."

The secret is found in the smaller chip technology that has filled the world with over 6 billion *non-computer* chips. "If current rates continue, there will be some 10 billion tiny grains of silicon chips embedded into our environment by 2005," writes Kevin Kelly, executive editor for *Wired* magazine and author of NEW RULES FOR THE NEW ECONOMY.

"We're sitting on the cusp of the post-PC era," notes IBM's general manager of the Pervasive Computing division, Mark Bregman. "Chips are getting so small and inexpensive that it's possible to place them in everything — in clothes, in cars, in household appliances."

In fact, the chip industry has become so ubiquitous that, according to Bregman, the city of Paris "is planning to put chips in all of its 90,000 trees in order to monitor health and age statistics."

Trans-World
Monitor
Reviewing World News of a World in Transition

Produced through the auspices of
Transition Research, Inc.
P. O. Box 42005
Houston, TX 77242
713/782-1304
Please call for subscription information